LEADERSHIP/
FOLLOWERSHIP

MARK LEE

LEADERSHIP/ FOLLOWERSHIP

Horizon House Publishers
Beaverlodge, Alberta, Canada

To

HUGH HUMPHRIES
PAUL KRESS
NORMAN COSAND
Colleagues, Friends,
Gentlemen, Christians
—members of the Simpson College Cabinet

© 1983
Horizon House Publishers
All Rights Reserved

ISBN 0-88965-062-4 (paperback)

HORIZON BOOKS
are published by Horizon House Publishers
Box 600, Beaverlodge, Alberta TOH OCO
Printed in the United States of America

Contents

About the Author

Mark W. Lee has been President of Simpson College, San Francisco since 1970. Previous to that, he taught at Whitworth College in Spokane, Washington, and at Northwestern College in St. Paul, Minnesota.

While serving at Whitworth, he earned the Ph.D. degree in 1966 from the University of Washington (Rhetoric and Public Address). Previous education includes a diploma from Nyack College, Nyack, New York; B.A. and M.A. degrees from Wheaton College, Wheaton, Illinois; and graduate studies at the University of Minnesota.

Dr. Lee is the author of several books, including *Our Children: Our Best Friends*, *Creative Christian Marriage*, *How to Set Goals and Really Reach Them*, *Who Am I and What Am I Doing Here*, and *Humor Is No Laughing Matter*. His lectures are sold in cassette tapes under the LeeSon label. Articles he has written have appeared in several journals and magazines.

A busy speaker, Dr. Lee has spoken in as many as twenty-seven states and Canada in a single year. For a number of years he spoke to radio audiences on several sustained broadcast series. *Conference Echoes* broadcasts some of his addresses over Family Stations, Inc.

He has served as consultant in communications and management for a number of institutions and industries, including such varied groups as Standard Oil of California, IBM, Credit Union Leagues, the Administrative Management Society, the Veterans Administration, the Civil Service Commission, and a number of state departments, federal agencies, professional organizations and denominations of churches.

Dr. Lee and his wife, Fern, reside in San Francisco. They have four children, Sharon, Mark Jr., David and Rachel Jody (all adults), and eight grandchildren.

Preface

In depression days, when even adolescents could not afford bicycles or bats and balls, we used to play "Follow the Leader." It was an easy game, sometimes great fun. The leader, depending upon his peculiar tastes, would run, jump, fall, skid, roll, creep, leap, and we would follow him, doing whatever he did. If a follower failed, he went to the end of the line. Sometimes we would jump a fence, leap a bush, run down a stream, crawl over a trestle, and run a marathon to keep up with the leader and finish with him. Some dropped out. Some missed portions of events. Others fell far behind. On rendezvous, the followers nearest the leader were chosen to become the next leaders. If enough boys were present, one team would challenge the other. The game, for leaders and followers, was strenuous. Decades later, I wonder if there is anything of that old game left in me as I ponder principles of leadership and followership.

No person is a leader without at least one follower, and there is no follower without at least one leader. Neither followership nor leadership will be rightly perceived without understanding both.

For some reason, perhaps the pride of man, leadership is generally valued more highly than followership. Leaders get publicity. To follow is often viewed as somewhat demeaning, or perhaps inferior to leading. This is false, of course. Superior virtue does not accrue to

9

leaders, inferior virtues to followers—though we do hope for excellent role models in leaders.

Much of popular belief about Christian leadership and followership is distortion of both. For some persons, authoritative and submissive conduct is all they perceive for leaders and followers. But the leader may not be a commander; he may be an example, having no authority whatever except his ability to inspire people to take a different life course. Moreover, not everyone, not even many, need to follow an individual in order for him to be a leader. The follower is not simply the lowly worker, a respondent to commands. He may be a person who takes creative ideas and, by creative means, accomplishes a task, calling upon others to join. In choosing a leader, a follower may take on responsibility to lead others through to the end of the assignment. Leadership/followership involves dynamics not easily coded.

 A prevailing viewpoint in this writing is that there are many types of leadership. A person may succeed in one situation and fail totally in another because the two situations are different. Ulysses S. Grant, so excellent a general in the American Civil War, may have become the poorest leader of all presidents of the United States. In the Scriptures, the leadership of David, the king, in consolidating the kingdom, required military prowess. Solomon, David's son and successor, easily outdid his father in maintaining peace and national solidarity. Both were significant leaders, but quite different.

The point to be made is that each situation requires leadership/followership suited to that situation. Humanly speaking, there is no one person for all seasons.

Our purpose here is to discover, through biblical principles and narratives, through supportive human theories and historical experience, what leadership and followership may be. We seek to translate the ancient biblical castings into modern perceptions. In this way, we may come to know in what ways we wish to lead, if we will and can, and in what ways we wish to follow. Opportunity to do either determines a part of our response. There are times to lead and times to follow, and both are periodic options for us. They provide or deny opportunities.

Perhaps as Christians we wish to know what leaders and followers are, so that we may be obedient to God's expectations about our roles. Fulfilling both roles is vital to personal and institutional success. Any person closely related to family and church life knows that absence of leaders and/or followers is catastrophic. If we should address issues of schools, business and government, we would make a similar statement about the loss to institutions when leadership/followership fails. Modern national family life appears to be in serious jeopardy, in part for failure of both leadership and followership of the most constructive kinds.

My acknowledgements in the preparation of this manuscript belong primarily to two persons. All other acknowledgements are found in the text or citations of borrowed materials. For well over a decade, Yvonne Cederblom has served magnificently as my secretary. She seems to be an indefatigable typist, and her work has been the best I have ever observed. My wife has, beyond my first professional expectations, become supportive of my work. Her sacrifice of our time, her reading of my materials, and her suggestions are greatly valued. Without the support of these two persons in skills and other ways as well, I could not reach my extensive goals. Indeed, without them the goals would not have been designed.

Further, the support of the Board of Trustees of Simpson College in my work and ministry since my entrance to the administration of the college has made possible the most productive and gratifying period of my life. They deserve my appreciation. In addition, Neill

Foster and Eric Greenway of Horizon House Publishers have made their publication and editing professionally competent, a matter of ministry. Their encouragement and assistance have been necessary ingredients in my work, under this title and others.

—1—

The Possibility of Leadership
OPPORTUNITY

David said moreover, the Lord that delivered me out of the paw of the lion, and out of the paw of the bear, he will deliver me out of the hand of this Philistine. And Saul said unto David, Go, and the Lord be with thee.

—*1 Samuel 17:37*

So he shepherded them according to the integrity of his heart, And guided them with his skillful hands.

—*Psalm 78:72, NASB*

We need to rescue the Old Testament from children. Because the stories of Moses in Midian and Egypt, or Daniel in the lions' den, or Jonah and the great fish, or David before the giant have been cast in children's idioms, almost in mythological terms, adults often do not feel the force of whole biblical biographies as genuine human experiences.

These biographical reviews and others teach much about God and leadership/followership. Moses did perform valiantly to become Israel's savior from slavery in Egypt. Israel did show up in Palestine, journeying from Egypt. David stood as a man before Goliath, youthful, but not a curly-headed boy with a toy slingshot; he was not an ancient Tom Sawyer. David did consolidate the kingdom of Israel. Daniel did survive a den of lions, but he, as well as others, accomplished much more in holding together a captive people.

Most leaders/followers in the Bible are studies of success and failure. Elijah did succeed in radically changing the life of all Israel at Carmel. He cut and ran afterward, yielding his position to Elisha. Jonah was a real prophet, with a genuine life mission, but he performed poorly in the Nineveh assignment. His larger ministry, unknown to us, must have been honorable and effective. If not, he would not have been called for the Nineveh campaign. Outside his home province he failed in leadership.

These, and other leading Old Testament characters, sometimes with less dramatic experiences, teach us much about practical, effective leadership, especially spiritual leadership. That spiritual leadership, taken together with practical application of it, is the main issue we seek to understand out of this writing. We will look at the leadership qualities in David, Moses, Nehemiah, Paul, and others. Non-biblical characters are also important here as citations. Their experiences are informative in a review of the never-ending need for leadership.

We also need to remind ourselves of the historicity of the New Testament. Jesus did accomplish His miracles and preach His sermons. Paul survived life threats to plant churches at least as far away as Spain. They and many others inform us about leadership that changed the world. Some failed, some succeeded, and most alternated between failure and success; but success as contemporaries, in their age or ours, define it is not guaranteed to leaders. The information and principles they left to us are practicable for our day. They beg for interpretation in our time.

Our concern here is with leadership/followership — principally but not exclusively in Christian meanings. The Bible, Old and New Testaments, has much to say about it. Here we take all Scripture seriously. From it we gain our life theory and, for this purpose, examples on leadership/followership. We ask standard questions about the Scriptures and our specific subject. We cut into the text at nearly any point, and relevant issues appear from it on our theme. Those issues deserve our sharp attention, especially in times when society seems uncertain about roles and directions for its people.

In treating our subject, we will usually divide the ideas of leadership and followership in order to keep the concepts clear. Ideally we would not speak about one without the accompaniment of the other. But much of what is written here will be in the terms of leadership. Followership is strongly implied in that material. Leadership calls for response.

Following Jesus is a major New Testament focus. Following firmly implies leadership. Jesus called His disciples to His leadership by saying, at the appropriate time, "Come and follow me." Later, the apostle Paul repeated, "Be ye followers of me as I am of Christ." Considerable biblical teaching relates to leadership and followership, as well as the making of leaders and followers.

Opportunity

Does a situation call out a leader, or does a leader make a situation? A study of more than a score of leaders in the book of Judges suggests that circumstances generate leaders. In contrast, the succession of kings following the period of the judges implies ongoing royal leadership regardless of circumstances. In analysis of American presidents, similar questions about priority of leaders or circumstances recur in historical analyses. Did Lincoln become great, as other men might have, because of the circumstances of the American Civil War? Or, would the president, entirely on his own, have demonstrated leadership greatness, war or no war?

Our general conclusion is that man and society always need leadership. At times special and dynamic leadership is required. Other occasions require only management leadership. Men and circumstances go together. Problems put men and women on trial. No analyst can be sure of the competence of untried persons.

Opportunity calls for leadership, but many candidates for leadership do not perceive opportunity. Stories, ancient and modern, compel speculation about opportunity. One wonders what might have happened if Jonathan had accepted David's proposal to join his administration. Jonathan chose not to accept the opportunity; he died with his father in battle. What might have happened had Lot dutifully followed Abraham, his uncle, until he would have received the Abramic business and power? What happened if Timothy was patient to the end of the apostle Paul's life? Did he take up the ministry of the supreme missionary that his mentor had willed to him?

Modern stories of missed opportunities intrigue us. A friend of Henry Ford's rejected the opportunity to participate with Ford in the founding of a motor company. The rejection was a monumental error in judgment.

A man I knew well in my youth, Harry Seager, never forgot his missed opportunity and often repeated his story. When I knew Seager, during the great depression of the 1930s, he was a fish salesman, peddling his product daily to small neighborhood grocery stores. He eked out his living, satisfactory for depression days, as best he could. But when he was a young man, he knew a dynamic fellow who proposed that Seager join him in a venture to package yeast for sale in stores. The man believed that, with the growth of cities, the rural family habit of saving yeast dough for each ensuing day's baking would prove inconvenient. New uses were proposed for the product as well, such as taking it as a food supplement. (Vitamin pills later replaced it.) Perhaps three to five cents' charge for a cube of yeast would make the public change habits. Cheap and readily available, yeast could make the two men rich. However, Seager turned down the opportunity. His friend, a man by the name of Fleischmann, proceeded to establish a business in his own name and became a millionaire.

A Biblical Example of Opportunity

Biblical perceptions for analyzing leadership opportunity may be extracted from David's experience with

Goliath. A lengthy Bible chapter, 1 Samuel 17, chronicles the event. Israelites and Philistines were entrenched against each other. A warrior, Goliath, impressive in physical stature, challenged the Israelites to send a champion against him. No Israelite accepted. Both military lines held, unwilling to attack or surrender. An opportunity was obvious for someone, presumably a soldier.

In that ancient time, soldiers were provisioned by their families. Three of Jesse's sons served in Saul's army, with their youngest brother, David, oscillating between home and battleground, taking provisions and returning with news of both the welfare of his brothers and progress of the war. David, on this occasion, organized his home obligations as he always did, and took the provisions from Jesse's larder to the camp. On arrival, in conversation with his brothers and other soldiers, he learned about Goliath and his challenge.

David sought further information. He quickly raised questions about the situation, what the circumstances were, the spiritual interests pertaining, and the rewards for taking this risk. He carefully collected facts by which he could decide his part in the campaign. His brothers criticized his involvement. Undeterred, he defended his question technique to his brothers, who attempted to put him down. Other soldiers, hearing about his interest and attitude, reported to Saul. Invited into the king's presence, David discussed the problem. Saul accepted the plan for confronting Goliath prescribed by David. At the moment, for Saul, there appeared nothing better to do. David's proposal was not silly. It would be worth a try, better than nothing.

David designed a strategy. Knowing his own skills, and having full confidence in them, David walked toward the Philistine lines, holding his shepherd's stick in full view. As he approached Goliath, he picked up five smooth stones from the torrent bed. To the giant the weapon was the stick, but David's *strategy* was found in the slingshot. Had Goliath perceived that strategy, he would have been less confident. Goliath would likely have protected himself, not an impossible task.

The opportunity for leadership was presented on David's visit to the lines. David would not have accepted the challenge without knowledge and an effective plan to meet it. Goliath was felled by a stone bullet, shot from the sling of the young shepherd. The Philistines fled. Israel's army pursued, defeating the Philistines and winning a significant victory. David became a standard leader of soldiers in the ensuing rout and fighting.

Appearing in the story are: opportunity, leadership, strategy or plan, implementation, and follow-through. There are also consequences of victory for David and Israel, including personal reward and occupational assignment for David. Israel won the war. David soon became an active officer in Saul's army and a hero among the people. Responding to opportunity, David was dramatically relocated from the farm to the battlefield. A sequence of events began that would give him the kingship of all Israel. (One wonders which brother returned to his father's home to manage and work Jesse's estate. David appears to have been required to take more than his turn between wars.)

Persons who lead earn the right to lead as they respond appropriately to meaningful opportunities. The young David seems to have learned leadership lessons at each juncture of his life reported in the Old Testament. His songs suggest that the knowledge he gained through his experiences was stored for a later period. This application may be the essence of wisdom. Even as a follower, dutifully serving the directives of his father, David learned skills he would utilize for leadership. He referred to the strategies of his lonely vigils with sheep as useful to leadership and victory. Other biblical characters followed similar dramatic opportunities to leadership; Abraham, Joseph and Moses provide significant cases in point.

Tracing leaders' experiences backward, if we can, to the beginning of their emergence, may be enlightening. Working backward from the height of David's reign as king in Israel, the opportunities, and what David did with them during the early years, become clear and impressive. Much of David's experience seems orderly, particularly suited to our search for principles of leadership/followership. David's life suggests to us how we may identify leaders. This identity matter is an important one.

An insurmountable problem for one man is an opportunity for another. This difference in personal viewpoint relates to leadership potential. David's brothers, like many men in any era, appear to have been waiting for "lightning to strike." That was fantasy. They hoped the Philistines would go away, that Goliath might have an accident, or that strong allies would aid Israel. But David viewed the problem, not as something that might go away or something that someone else should confront, but as an opportunity requiring action from him.

Life's steps are seldom taken two or three at a time. Rather, each step prepares us for the next one. Each invites us to consider something more. Application of ourselves at each step is key. Application is opportunity-taking, and that requires studied and orderly action if there is hope for success. Only a few persons are on the "fast track," skipping steps here and there along the way. Commonly there are more failures, even tragedies, on that track than most of us would countenance. Of course, there are exotic exceptions—but we are concerned here with standard patterns. What is usually the case?

Modern Life Opportunity

When the early church evaluated potential leaders, the members were advised to review their family life as a starting point. If a man demonstrated leadership with his family, he might well provide leadership in the church (1 Tim. 3). The progression was, and continues to be, clear. Leadership in one area implies, but does not guarantee, effective leadership in another. People have to start someplace. Family leadership success or failure is no guarantee for other success or failure, but a tendency has been noted with the family experience.

Absence of leadership in a person for one area of opportunity gives reason for pause in making assignments to another for him. Perhaps the emergence of the apostle Paul was partly delayed because his "track record" was not appealing to the church. It appeared he might lead to destroy. Could he lead to heal?—to advance?—to achieve?

In the end, Paul's leadership proved to be different from that of the other disciples. His experiences among leaders of orthodox Jewry made it different. The other disciples were largely from peasant background; then they experienced disciple preparation with Jesus (2 Cor. 11-12). Paul's education was in a formal setting, among the leaders of power. There were personal differences as well. Paul's reference to his own singleness in contrast to Peter's lifestyle, which included travel with a wife, is a glimpse of one of those differences (1 Cor. 9). Paul appears to have taken greater risks than married men might be expected to take. He set out on an adventure of leadership that could not be fitted into family models. He implied as much in First Corinthians, chapter seven.

The rule for any prospective leader is to order his life, take appropriate opportunities, and follow a leadership route to the acceptable goal. Before entering college, I fairly well projected what I would do with my life. My projections were modest at first, but having any projections at all vaulted me ahead of that static experience I, and my friends, had made out of high school. At this juncture in my life I am appalled at my own neglect as a young person, and amazed at the oversights of youths noted in my observations and travels. In some way their elders seem not to be doing all they should do to help them find direction.

As I grew older each opportunity was taken as I perceived each, with available energy and enthusiasm. So many places of learning for leadership were lost to me in high school because I could "get by." So I was not elected, not asked, not pushed forward. Some gratifying things were done, but they were modest achievements when contrasted with the possibilities. In college I was elected to the presidency of my sophomore class; in the next college, to the presidency of the student body. During student days many other opportunities appeared and were taken. I learned from each, sometimes through failure, or through holding patterns, or through legitimate advance. My life became more exciting. I began to take some risk (promise but no assurance, and with some possibility of failure), and it was good. Opportunities for leadership, with their creativity and learning, increased. In retrospect I am astonished by the differences between early oversights and later privileges. In some way those differences ought to be articulated to youths whose productive lives are ahead of them. For me they related importantly to my own perceptions and conduct before it was too late to participate.

During this development period, I read the remarks of many acknowledged leaders. Some of them stated clearly, but in their own way, what I suspected to be the case: prepare and believe your opportunity will come. Abraham Lincoln said that he would study and get ready—"Perhaps my time will come." He did get ready. His time did come. He, like David, prepared himself, using the accumulated wisdom of experiences he had or knew about.

LEADERSHIP USES ORDER
LEADING TO OPPORTUNITY (1 Sam. 17:20-22)

To a degree each of us is influenced by the progression of experiences in his life. We believe that order emerges from whatever precedes our current circumstances. This is basic to decision making. We begin with what we have and proceed to the next event. As noted above, life's steps are seldom taken two at a time, much less three or four at a time. Each step, when we follow order, prepares us for consecutive ones.

We must be wise enough to recognize this orderliness. Our activities are not, or should not be, random ones. Disorder in activities may become, as Shakespeare said of a man's thoughts and language, "like tangled chains, nothing impaired, but all disordered." Activities ought to be used as links in forging our straight life chain. With recognition of this pattern, we must find the vision and energy to apply ourselves to make each link strong and related.

If I am to lead effectively, that leadership must grow out of the experiences I have had. My preparation for and practice of speaking, preaching and teaching provide key information both to others and myself about me. My past becomes an effective indicator of the type of leadership I may provide in the future. Because my life has been professionally committed to teaching college students, principally in church-related schools, and preaching or speaking to adult groups, it is likely that I can lead most effectively when those factors may be incorporated into, or perceived in some way useful to, the leadership that is needed from me.

Part of my life plan was to become a leader in my own

selection of educational and church institutions. That meant there were limitations that ordered my approach to possible future opportunities. Because church people, in evangelical environments, respond to different criteria than, say, standard labor union members, my development was cast in patterns meaningful to my ultimate purposes. The schools I selected, the internships I took, the readings and experiences I sought, were related to the ultimate goal of leading responsibly in a Christian evangelical environment.

When the early church sought leadership, and much of it was needed at the outset, an orderly, practical approach was made to the matter. Churches were given a list of criteria that were to characterize their leaders. This was vital because moral uprightness was a necessary characteristic of Christian leadership. Some factors were negative (no brawler, not given to wine), and some affirmative (temperate, prudent, respectable). And there were social factors of a general nature that would suggest potential leadership qualities—he would be a leader in his family, if he had a family. If the man could be accepted as a leader by his wife and children, this might commend him as a potential candidate for social and spiritual leadership. Such an affirmation was no guarantee, as suggested earlier. But it was a starting point in the identification process.

A person is developing leadership potential as he responds effectively to each venture in his life. He builds a bank of confidence both in himself and with others. As a follower he is preparing to lead followers. As a general rule this preparation is an important factor for leadership. Students wisely learn the rule already cited: "Get ready, and your time will come." It is a basic presupposition used by most college counselors no matter what the nature of their institutions.

David, the shepherd son and later king, appears to have

developed an order that he followed meticulously, learning from each experience. He demonstrated obedience to his father and family. The Bible reader is impressed by his industry. Each scene has David carrying more than normal responsibility, other family members less. David could either complain about the injustices of the volume of his assignments, or he could learn something in carrying them out. He chose the latter.

Were it not for his strategies with Saul on the visit to the front lines during the Goliath challenge, we might believe that David was merely a hardworking youngest son, partly exploited by his family. It may be that the biblical record is highly selective, providing an illusion to us about David's industry, but the illusion holds nonetheless. David certainly proved that he knew what followership was, and that he could follow well. Only when he emerges in the events leading up to confrontation with Goliath do we learn that David has been preparing for opportunity. As noted earlier, his brothers seemed sometimes to be waiting for lucky situations.

We know the course by which David ultimately made the decision to confront the Philistine champion. His motives were mixed. That made him human enough. Certainly he was zealous for God, and readily affirmed his spiritual confidence and reliance. David met with King Saul and analyzed him, as we later discover. Saul, never really confident in his royal role, became sensitive to the rights of office. As incompetency reveals itself in an individual, he may become jealous for and protective of his status. He invents means for holding on. Saul did that. Even though Saul promised his daughter to David as part of motivation to lead a military expedition, David appeared to be reluctant, casting his arguments in humble denials—he was unworthy to be admitted into the royal family. It may have been disarming to Saul. David anticipated Saul's jealousy toward him and retreated diplomatically.

Almost from the beginning Saul felt threatened by young David. David appears to have perceived that Saul would not maintain objective friendship and support. The events are dramatic. The king's duplicity is quickly revealed by the initial offer of his eldest daughter, Merab, to David. David demurs about becoming the king's son-in-law. He is astute beyond his years. He does not have a popular base large enough to challenge Saul, but large enough that Saul must act cautiously with him. Saul is confident the Philistines will dispose of David. Merab is given to another suitor. It is likely that David is not really interested in Merab. Michal, another daughter of Saul, loves David, and her affection is apparently reciprocated. David appears, on the surface, to lose in the political moves. But he does not lose. He knows what he is about, and wins.

Saul, willing to exploit his daughter Michal, sets up an ambitious military proposal calling for the deaths of one hundred enemies of Israel. Their deaths, presumably beneficial to Israel, will earn for the champion the hand of Michal. Saul fully expects David to lose his life in the venture. Again, David turns the risk into opportunity. Succeeding, he becomes Saul's son-in-law through marriage to Michal. Becoming a member of the royal family, David is never genuinely accepted by Saul.

Saul failed in leadership. He attempted to destroy or dilute leadership potential in others. His real duty was to develop it in himself and others for the benefit of the kingdom. He failed in his analysis and use of men. His own jealousy, a self-made enemy for any leader, cost him the support of competent men. Had he positioned David, and understood the quality of the young man, Saul would have enjoyed a superior administration. He feared competition. However, David was a man able to serve well even an incompetent leader. Saul never saw that, did not believe it was possible.

Much of the evil in Saul, deplored by Samuel, was in Saul's pride, suspicion, lack of leadership confidence and especially his loss of spiritual integrity. Ultimately these factors became intense. Saul appears to have become schizophrenic. He lost the meaning of the order of events in his life and in that of the nation. It was only a matter of time until this king would lose his kingdom. At first, part fell to David. Eventually David ruled all Israel. Some time before he lost the last battles of his life for his divided realm, Saul distorted the leadership qualities that had elevated him at the beginning. Even his son, Jonathan, perceived the tragedy of his father.

LEADERSHIP FINDS MEANING IN
EVENTS FOR OPPORTUNITY (1 Sam. 17:36)

We learn from Scripture that God specializes in using whatever is available. That perception is illustrated in the stories of Moses with a stick, Shamgar with an ox-goad, Gideon with a pitcher, and David with a slingshot. It should not be our purpose to insist on resources unavailable to us, but to utilize effectively what we have or can get with reasonable effort.

David's experience illustrates an attempt by others to make a leader in an image not his own. Discussing the circumstances of the Goliath threat, Saul proposes to turn David into an instant soldier and officer. Saul's own armor, helmet, shield and sword were provided. Perhaps in deference to the king, David buckled on the uniform and found poor fit. Saul, a physically big man, perhaps the largest soldier in both lines except for Goliath, confused status with ability, leadership with the accoutrements of leadership, and size with power.

David could lead as David, not as Saul. He would not

become a "ninety-minute wonder." If he did, he would lose. He could be a shepherd-leader, relating his experience to the problem at hand. In adding up the circumstances, he could propose to approach the crisis as he saw it. It turns out that his was a special way, but for him it was standard. His past experience of dropping a strong, fast-moving animal with a stone, firmly and accurately slung, was evidence enough for David that a slow-moving, ponderous giant might be stopped.

Saul and his officers were not creatively leading their troops. They thought in terms of traditional battles. They were now faced with a new kind of situation requiring a new solution. They were paralyzed, not merely with fear but with the failure of leadership. Analyzing the circumstances, they might have, as leaders, designed new strategies to lead. They needed what all leaders must possess, a belief that the problem before them can be solved. Concern should be with creativity, strategy, timing, personnel, energy and materials. And, we remember, there is risk.

If I am a leader I must know what personal tools are available to me and put them to work. One leader possesses charisma, an attractive and dynamic personality. He will be wise to use that tool. But he lacks education, and education may be necessary to carry through his assignment. He may seek education, if opportunity and time permit. Or he may educate himself on how to use educated people. He may not have all necessary resources in himself, so he mobilizes those who do. This is high evidence of his leadership ability.

Biblical concepts of leadership tell us a great deal about modern situations in which prospective leaders find themselves. What happened when something was missing in the ancient leader? When potential leaders in the Bible tried to avoid their own leadership, they were sometimes persuaded. The miracles of Moses were given only because of his reticence in going to Egypt under standard circumstances. His rod-to-serpent-to-rod, and the hand-to-leprosy-to-restoration were as much to convince Moses as the Egyptians. Moses could lead through a wilderness, not because he was a king, but because he was a shepherd. A king would have failed in forty years in that wilderness.

David would have lost if he had approached Goliath in any other way than as an effective defender of sheep. David's confidence commended him for future experiences. Instead of deploring his circumstances, he used what was available to him. Were his resources unsatisfactory, he would not have taken on the giant warrior. And he did have Israel's army behind him for support.

Some persons, potentially effective leaders, back away because of lack of education, lack of complete resources, or lack of something else. They may be wise to back away as long as they feel as they do.

Their reticence implies that they would not lead well, even if endued with any gift or talent provision they request. Saul would have done well to have made stick his initial reluctance to be appointed. His physical appearance, so attractive to people, was not enough to make a king.

As already noted, leadership in the biblical context tends to use what is available or can become available. If I am a leader, I must use whatever tools are mine. For David, the tools were those of a shepherd, skillfully handled. He did not have the skills of a soldier—not yet. He was not a lawyer, an architect, an engineer, or a sailor. He would not choose to be captain of a ship in a storm at sea.

In the Scriptures there are principles of progression that appeal to prospective leaders, at least appeal to those who are faith-oriented in their view of things. If the prospective leader gains God's approval in the first small opportunity, he moves to another and higher plateau—and onward after that. For David, a rabbit precedes the lion, and the lion precedes the giant Goliath. Men of faith tend to build on an order of events, from the smaller (like the effective treatment of family), to the larger (like the church). The Bible principle is that faithfulness in small matters precedes the privilege of serving in larger ones that lead to reward.

LEADERSHIP DISCOVERS OBSTACLES THAT BLOCK OPPORTUNITY

Goliath was not the real obstacle. He provided an opportunity for leadership on the part of Israel. The fear and lack of creativity in Israel's king and soldiers were the obstacles. David sensibly took time preparing himself for the decision to accept or reject the opportunity. Could he disregard the resistance, criticism and jealousy of his brothers? Could he gain Saul's support? Could he treat the crisis in his own way? Could he succeed with the first shot, or would he need to parry his enemy for several shots? What part would God accept in the venture? These were David's relevant questions. To meet the obstacles he responded to his brothers, reviewed strategies with Saul, collected five stones, and "psyched himself up" for the ordeal. He sought spiritual energy and confidence.

Each person trying to lead may expect to encounter sufficient resistance to discourage him. Leaders or potential leaders sometimes capitulate to various discouragements and turn away from opportunities. A series of matters, taken together, may discourage anyone and block opportunity. Persons start well, encounter resistance, and withdraw. It is a common pattern caused by fear, not as much for self as for failure. Failure causes loss of face. And loss of face, we fear, may end opportunities for us.

FIGURE ONE
Obstacles that block opportunity

1. Publicity

The leader is misrepresented before the public

2. Size of problem

The perceived magnitude of the problem causes the leader's supporters to retreat.

3. Bureaucracy

A burden of controls prevents leadership from utilizing ideas and resources.

4. Erosion of authority

Absence or loss of authority on the part of the leader causes delay or failure.

5. Factionalism

Human differences create factions, problem-solving activity ceases, and the opportunity is lost.

6. Homogenization

Excellence in leadership is rejected; the mediocrity in leadership that results fails to solve large problems.

7. Intolerance

A leader becomes the object of character assassination, party spirit, threats, suspicion, disdain or physical attacks.

8. Fears

Fear of failure, criticism or error drains leaders and followers of the confidence needed to take advantage of opportunities.

9. Motivations

Over-emphasis on personal reward leads to rejection of opportunities.

10. Lack of creativity

Various blocks to creativity preclude the appropriation of opportunities.

Publicity

Prospective leaders are sometimes discouraged by mis-representation of themselves or their followers by others. At times simple gossip strings out and grows into a large web, focusing bad light on a man or his cause. By this device leaders have been weakened beyond ability to function effectively. In current times one observes this often, on small and large scales. In electronic media reporters are concerned with conflict, seldom with consensus. In some areas the repetition of an issue, or accent on even a minor factor, can so distort the point of concern, or discourage the leader, that the case is lost, leadership fails. Such was the case when David, after some years of reign, was undermined by his son, Absalom. Absalom, by force of his own personality, distracted the loyalty of the people from David to himself. He did it by a gossip system that became difficult to overcome. It led to a short, bloody uprising.

A destructive aspect of reporting is that even its volume — whether too much or too little — overemphasizes or underemphasizes points of leadership or issues of importance. Too much sun makes a desert, too little a tundra. Too much reporting of the McCarthy activities in the United States during the early 1950s contributed to the professional destruction of some leaders and followers. A competent senator from Maryland lost an election because of temporary fear in the citizenry created by the publicity-seeking senator from Wisconsin, Joseph McCarthy. It is possible, then, to destroy good leaders and for citizens to accept inferior leadership. The best leaders have no assurance of their own success. That is part of the risk they take to lead. The jungle sometimes eats them up.

Size of Problem

On occasion an obstacle to leadership is the size of the

problem. If the problem is perceived to be too large, people retreat. They fear failure and do not wish to risk it. For this reason some institutions that should not fail do fail because prospective leaders back away from what might well have been saved with their help. In such a situation the leader *falls* rather than *fails*. David's plan to rid himself of Uriah, Bathsheba's husband, is a case in point. Uriah, an eminent officer, fell because his own men retreated from him; he could not prevail alone against a regiment.

On several occasions I have observed colleges fail or nearly fail when a few trustees or administrators backed away from difficult or knotty situations. Afraid of sharing the blame for failure, or afraid of the volume of work necessary for the survival of the institution, they withdrew, making the inherent threat more severe. They sometimes made their predictions of failure self-fulfilling. They quit. Then the leader had fewer troops, perhaps too few. Even the strategies of Robert E. Lee, that genius of the Confederate armies, failed before the greater numbers of soldiers and superior firepower available to the Northern armies.

To be sure, there are situations in which the problem is excessive for immediately available leadership. In such instances other leadership and resources must be sought. The leader of an institution evaluated one of his subordinates in this way: "He is a fine fellow, but he is a .20 calibre pistol in a .38 calibre situation." They had to find another leader, moving this one to lesser responsibility. Twenty calibres are better than thirty-eights in some situations.

Bureaucracy

A common obstacle to opportunity is the burden of controls and interference from others, preventing leadership from utilizing ideas and resources. The committee approvals required, the volume of paperwork to be completed, the number of managers to be cleared, the stack of amendments added to a plan, may well dilute or destroy any opportunity. Openings to it are blocked, not with necessary matters to be met before the opportunity is seized, but with obstacles which, even if surmounted, add nothing constructive to the product or solution.

If a committee is unnecessary, one should not be used just to comfort those who wish to have all democratic procedures included. In the name of democracy many false gestures are made. The action is a charade and diminishes respect for both democracy and potential opportunity. It is to be remembered, however, that the leader respects democratic principles and can differentiate them from bureaucratic interferences.

Erosion of Authority

Authority has fallen upon bad reputation. Resistance to authority by citizens is commonplace, beginning with lack of respect for authority. It is said that loss of respect by American soldiers for their officers, a loss that began in earnest during the 1950s in the Korean conflict, and broke into the open during the Vietnam war, ultimately took effect at most levels of civilian life. Authority breakdown has taken place in most contexts: parent/child, student/teacher, worker/supervisor, citizen/public official.

Authority sometimes declines in groups or institutions almost to the point of extinction. When it does, opportunity may have to wait, or be approached in new and creative ways acceptable to all. These ways are often slower. For without effective authority, leadership is slowed. It may not accomplish its purpose. If leadership begins with authority, and later finds that authority either taken away or sufficiently diminished, the leader will commonly back away, or totally disassociate himself. Wisely, he leaves the field. Others are left to sift out circumstances. In large and small situations authority must usually be granted to someone to get things done. In leadership there should be at least basic authority to command where necessary. Without it there will at least be delay, perhaps failure.

Factionalism

A leader may be well on the way to capitalizing on an opportunity; a reasonable plan is complete and in place. But because human viewpoints inevitably differ, and some critics are unwilling to compromise, factions can easily form. If factions are large and forceful they can slow or stop problem solving activity related to the opportunity. Even small factions may stall the work of the leader. In instances the leader may be reduced to an umpire. To be a referee is sometimes legitimate work for a leader, but if it becomes too difficult to sift through the factionalism, and conflicts last for too long a time, the leader is neutralized. The opportunity may be lost; its time runs out.

Homogenization

If people downplay excellence they inherit mediocrity. Mediocrity is the best of the worst, and the worst of the best. Ultimately followers get the kind of leadership they demand and support. If their demands are low, or too political, they heap to themselves leaders with low qualifications. When the best is reduced somewhat in the belief that the worst is elevated somewhat, that type of leader must be a different type from the creative, dynamic, charismatic, orderly leader who takes on the whole opportunity available to him. The worst of the best and the best of the worst are the standards for homogenizing life to create sameness. It may treat small problems fairly well. It fails in the large.

Intolerance

Since ancient times leaders have sometimes been destroyed either through reputational or physical assassination. The Gracchi brothers served Rome before the birth of Jesus. The first brother was killed by political enemies. Later his brother, holding the same primary office, was also killed. More than two millennia later, President John Kennedy was assassinated. In the same decade his brother, Robert, aspiring to the same office as John, was also killed.

Attacks on American presidents are studies in intolerance. During the fifty years since Franklin Roosevelt ran for the presidency of the United States, every president has been the object of death threats. Gunshots were fired at Roosevelt, Truman, Kennedy, Ford and Reagan. Except in Ford's case, someone was wounded or killed in the assaults. Such intolerance, as vicious as it is, is less a problem for society than the unpublicized massive intolerance which shows itself in the day-by-day rejection of leadership and constructive guidance.

Certainly leaders and leadership must be evaluated, but character assassination, prejudice, party spirit, and the like are not objective evaluative techniques. We are rightly suspicious of some leaders, but we ought to maintain confidence in leadership of the right sort. Disdain of a leader must not become disdain of leadership.

Fears

If either the people or the leader falls to fear, an opportunity will likely be divided, if taken at all. To fear failure, or criticism, or errors will drain both leaders and followers of the confidence they need. They will evade problems and the related opportunities challenging them. A reader readily follows the inquiries and plans David made before going out against Goliath. David appears to have held no great fear for risks. He reviewed and evaluated them. On the other hand, the Israelite army and King Saul were paralyzed with fear. For them, fear meant that they could do nothing. The possibilities were interpreted as improbabilities. David's fears were partly managed by David's intense faith in God. But he was sufficiently in control of himself that he could look past fear to possibilities. Those possibilities became probabilities in his perception.

Each person may introduce personal blocks, preventing him from effectively treating opportunities. Pride takes some leaders out of the running. They are willing to take on only those projects that virtually guarantee success. But pride may put other leaders into the fray. There was a commendable pride in God and kingdom in David's approach to the Goliath threat. Confidence rightly directed must have some element of appropriate pride in it.

Motivations

A leader should consider all available factors not only to settle on strategies but also to determine whether or not there is good reason for him to take on this project at this time. But if he bases his commitment on selfish motivations only, he is unworthy as a leader.

As stated earlier, David's motives were mixed, as most motives seem to be. Put down by his brothers, David may have believed they would eat their words about him if he overcame the Philistine. But there was so much more than sibling rivalry here, and he would decide privately the personal issues. He inquired further about the reward for taking such a risk against the outsized warrior. Leaders always measure risk against the fruits of victory. In the case of the giant's defeat, the one succeeding would be given the daughter of the king in marriage, an act that would make him a prince. In addition, his father's house would be made free in Israel. That is to say, the property would be no longer taxable, the family would be free of certain governmental restrictions.

Then, too, there was honor. Personal honor, no doubt, but also the honor of God. This last was compelling to the idealistic David. Perhaps this motivation has been too greatly reduced in our time—that individuals will and ought to serve in vital roles because that service brings honor to God.

Various personal blocks in our lives prevent us from exercising leadership. We may demand too much for ourselves. Our overemphasis on monetary rewards, on easiness of effort, on psychic benefits may prevent us.

Many persons are unemployed because they refuse to work unless they receive a salary they consider adequate. For them the choice is all or nothing. They prefer welfare to menial labor or menial salary. And welfare is appropriate when the need for it is present. But in welfare there is no opportunity. Welfare provides a temporary holding pattern, while an opportunity is sought. Such individuals could volunteer. Few do. By proving their worth, their potential, they might create their own opportunities. The future appears full of those opportunities, to be taken when barriers are overcome. It was Francis Bacon who said, "Opportunity has a bald noodle behind, there is nothing to grasp."

Lack of Creativity

Safan-Gerard perceived five great blocks to creativity.* We might well propose these blocks as significant also to leadership and opportunity:

1) *Making something fit a preconceived idea.* Young

---

* Desy Safan-Gerard, "How to Unblock," **Psychology Today**, January 1978, pp. 81, 83, 86.

David refused to get caught up with only the military way to get at the giant. Both armies believed in banging swords against shields until one army held the field, a field bloody with the slain. Both armies would suffer enormously, but one would be declared victor. David preferred strategy to excessive bloodletting. Leaders are believers in alternatives. There are alternative ways of doing things, perhaps alternative results that are better than initial objectives. These persons have flexibility, a necessity for leadership in projects involving more than a few people.

2) *Forcing activity before one is ready.* David might not have succeeded in an earlier try. He waited for full preliminary experience, which he highly credited as reason now to joust with Goliath. An insightful leader knows his day. He is willing to take time for preparation. Most of those we admire as leaders are persons who did not have to have everything immediately. Leaders hold a sense of timing. A study of effective military leaders almost always is captivating in that they knew when to retreat, when to hold, when to advance. Among Lincoln's **generals, Grant has that sense, McClellan did not. For the Confederates, Lee's greatest weakness was the** determination to attack. His charges were always brave and sometimes foolhardy.

3) *Concerning himself with techniques so as to miss the new ideas and their flow.* David would have failed in encountering Goliath in Saul's armor, even if the armor had fit him. He did not get caught in the military machinery, but rather turned to fresh ideas and his own tests. He had more to offer than the old ways. He could not discuss them too widely. Old-timers would make fun. They were trapped in former ways. Leaders ask for what is applicable in this instance, and ask why it may be expected to work. What can be found we have not found heretofore?

4) *Setting expectations too high so as to assure dissatisfaction*. David relied heavily upon his faith in God at the beginning, and that reliance included faith in himself, the person God had made. He held no expectations for anything different from its habit from the army of Israel, or for support from his brothers. He, with God, was at the ready. David knew what he could do, how far he could commit himself. His expectations were fitting for himself, but not for the others. So they were not included. Later they would be.

Every person working with leaders must evaluate goals as they relate to resources, personnel and time restraints. No one can do everything, even everything he wants to do. Some fantasies are too great for realization in this or that context of our lives. Leadership deals with the art of the possible. Courage is not to be confused with folly. Leadership does not flirt with impossibilities. It is related to plausible futures.

FIGURE TWO

Blocks to creativity

(Safan-Gerard)

1. Making something fit a preconceived idea.
2. Forcing activity before one is ready.
3. Concerning oneself with technique so as to miss the new ideas and their flow.
4. Setting expectations too high so as to assure dissatisfaction.
5. Starting evaluation too soon, before the project is far enough along.

5) *Starting evaluation too soon, before the project is far enough along*. David did not permit himself the luxury of evaluating the size, quality, strategies of the army. He did not argue that once Goliath was out of the way there would remain a battle to be fought. Neither side would keep the promise of surrender when the joust of champions ended. Israel's army would be needed. And Israel fought a standard war with the Philistines immediately following Goliath's death. David became a major military leader in that rout.

The point is that the evaluation of David's act could not be fully made until the whole war was fought. That evaluation is interesting. Out of the war a battle cry became cause for Saul's jealousy of David, and was often repeated by the people of Israel:

> Saul has slain his thousands,
> And David his ten thousands.

Possibilities for leadership are nearly always present, in the nature of things. Most of us could lead in some way. Not all problems are cast in Goliathan dimensions. There are stray foxes, and a few jackrabbits to be confronted—perhaps a bear and a lion. Most problems affecting us directly are within our boundaries. They can be solved.

> So he shepherded them according to the integrity of his heart, and guided them with his skillful hands.
>   (Psalm 78:72, NASB)

—2—

The Price of Leadership
COSTS

Then Moses heard the people weep throughout their families, every man in the door of his tent: and the anger of the Lord was kindled greatly; Moses also was displeased.

And Moses said unto the Lord, Wherefore hast thou afflicted thy servant? and wherefore have I not found favor in thy sight, that thou layest the burden of all this people upon me?

Have I conceived all this people? have I begotten them, that thou shouldest say unto me, Carry them in thy bosom, as a nursing father beareth the sucking child, unto the land which thou swarest unto their fathers?

Whence should I have flesh to give unto all this people? for they weep unto me, saying, Give us flesh, that we may eat.

I am not able to bear all this people alone, because it is too heavy for me.

And if thou deal thus with me, kill me, I pray thee, out of hand, if I have found favour in thy sight; and let me not see my wretchedness.

And the Lord said unto Moses, Gather unto me seventy men of the elders of Israel, whom thou knowest to be elders of Israel, whom thou knowest to be the elders of the people, and officers over them; and bring them unto the tabernacle of the congregation, that they may stand there with thee.

And I will come down and talk with thee there: and I will take of the spirit which is upon thee, and will put it upon them; and they shall bear the burden of the people with thee, that thou bear it not thyself alone.

—Numbers 11:10-17

Moses is the eminent biblical example of a leader loath to lead. There are others like Amos, or even Saul, the king. And human history records the names of reluctant princes. It appears that Jonathan did not relish the kingship of his father, Saul.

The model of many national leaders has been Cincinnatus, who agreed to leave his work, govern for a specified number of days in Rome, and return to his former labors. He kept his personal and public vow. He did not fall to the lure of power. When George Washington became president of the United States, he announced and later demonstrated the spirit of Cincinnatus in refusing a third term as chief executive. Returning to Mount Vernon, Washington finished out his life as he had lived it before the Revolution. His ideal to relinquish power after two terms as president held as the great American tradition until Franklin Roosevelt passed over it and ran for a third term in 1940, more than 150 years after Washington's first, and in the thirty-second administration of the American government. During the presidency of Harry Truman, Roosevelt's successor, two terms were made the legal standard.

During the experience of his call at the burning bush, Moses recited several reasons why he should not be constituted leader. The reasons and rationalizations were answered with argument and miracle to settle the reticent prophet. On the promise that Aaron, his brother, might accompany him and serve as dutiful spokesman, Moses relented. All his objections finally met, he responded to the directive for leadership.

That Moses grew in competence as a leader is clear from the record. Beginning reluctantly, with family breakup and fear about the entire venture, Moses seems to have quickly learned the lessons needed. From the experience at the bush until the commission of Joshua as successor forty years later, Moses became a masterful leader to the people. He overcame fear, false modesties, unworkable practices and policies, and other human weaknesses to forge a name for himself among eminent personages of all time. He has become a model for painters and sculptors who seek to create in their art the man Moses, larger than life, the activist friend of God, the giver of law basic to national codes and human morals.

Ultimately Moses knew his case. He recited it to Israel at the close of his ministry with them (Deut. 1:9-18). He admitted to them, at the time of his initiation, that he could not accomplish his assignment alone. God was the answer, so God must be honored. And what did God give to him and Israel? A plan of administration to authorize "wise, discerning and experienced men" from each tribe with authority to act. It began with family solidarity, with father leadership and responsibility. From small group organization, to larger, and ultimately to the whole of the nation, a special theocratic/democratic society was developed. Judgment was to be handled at as low level as possible, but could ultimately reach the supreme court, Moses, if the nature of a case justified it. All decision making was evenhanded, based on justice without special treatment.

So it was that out of personal weakness, (inability to bear the assignment of the burden of the people), came strength (the delegation of power to solve inevitable problems) and responsibility (to please God and see the venture through to the end). Shared leadership under law, a superior way to protect the rights of people, became a magnificent invention that introduced democracy to Israel. Admittedly it was a male dominated society, but was much ahead of the times in espousing human rights.

Whether one begins with Moses or with other idealistic leaders, he discovers similar characteristics in them. Those similarities provide strong corroboration for selecting Moses as our model. How did he meet the issues and solve them, conserving his own sanity? He, like others, encountered loneliness and weariness. He survived because he also had abandon and vision.

LEADERSHIP IMPOSES
LONELINESS (Numbers 11:10-17)

Loneliness is common accompaniment for leaders. It may be a by-product of leadership. Certainly Moses felt alone; but our judgment is not based completely on Moses' experience. The apostle Paul complained: "No one was with me." Especially do his later epistles imply that he felt alone, or that he had been abandoned, therefore alone. Jeremiah is remembered as a solitary figure, feeling he was abandoned, left utterly alone. Jeremiah is known as the "weeping prophet," a title partly earned because of his loneliness. Apparently he found abandonment too much to accept so joined Israel in captivity. Jonah was alone, a fact that may have contributed to his personal and spiritual problems. Elijah ran, and alone under the juniper tree reacted in ways that surprise us for a man of his experiential and faith dimensions. There was certainly loneliness in Jesus. We find Him in lonely vigils, and later complaining that three friends could not pray with him in Gethsemane. The leader oscillates between the marketplace with its

teeming crowds and the desert place where he stands
alone, and feels alone. In his loneliness there is reflection
and recharging of resources for the next duty.

When even a devout man or woman feels totally alone,
that person tends to feel separate from the earth, on
occasion so separated that he urges God to permit him to
die. He not only feels man forsakes him, but God's
ministry through him is ended. His response is to pray
God to take his life. He may complain, as Jonah and Elijah
did. There is the leader's presumption of unfairness, even
from God, in such cases; the duty or responsibility leaders
carry is not fairly balanced out with something else, like
honor, easier to bear.

Secular biography recites similar stories. Perhaps
Abraham Lincoln felt alone because of great waves of
personal depression, or his depressions may have been
triggered by his aloneness. Who can be sure? Scientists
like Columbus and Einstein appear to have walked at
times in life's lonely neighborhoods. Generals of armies
have written at length about the loneliness of command.
Modern space scientists speak openly of feeling alone in
working the great void of space. In Christian biography
the aloneness of David Brainerd, David Livingstone,
Albert Simpson and others is a feature in their life stories.

This loneliness may not be loneliness so much as
aloneness, the feeling that even when surrounded by
people one is not necessarily understood or supported in
carrying through the main purpose at hand. Even so, it is
a mystery that many leaders emerged from "alone" situations to lead. Moses spent forty years virtually alone as a
shepherd. How could it be otherwise for an adopted Egyptian prince? John the Baptist came alone out of the desert
and then elected disciples. David and Saul, first kings of
Israel, were "alone" men when we first discover them.

Leaders will likely feel lonely because followers are too
varied to embrace any leader's whole vision. Moses felt

the people imposed their burden on him, rather than help carry the divine one he had taken (Num. 11:11-12). Moses must have felt alone when his wife returned to her father, when Aaron failed him in the wilderness, and when Miriam found fault. In the end he was not entirely alone. He developed a team of leaders, at least seventy men, who assisted in carrying through the work. Even Jesus, often portrayed as a lonely figure, had many disciples. Loneliness is not unrelieved. A leader would not likely survive without some relief.

Spiritual leaders seem to experience a special aloneness. Daniel reported that, although other persons were with him on an occasion, they did not see the vision that he saw (Dan. 10:7-8). Jesus, at His baptism, heard words and responded to an experience that others nearby may have missed (John 1:29-33). The conversation between Saul of Tarsus and Jesus on the Damascus road made no sense to Saul's companions (Acts 9:7).

This loneliness is partly the loneliness of an achiever, and a person of vision. Pressing forward, he is not likely going to be fully understood. Awareness is not acute enough generally to cause men and women to enter even vicariously into the experiences of creative leaders. They may not wish to go beyond ordinary experiences. A.W. Tozer, writing in *Eternity* magazine, suggested that Enoch must have been lonely, and Noah too, and that with all Abraham had, God never spoke to him while he was in the presence of other men. Tozer then wrote that the "weakness of so many modern Christians is that they feel too much at home in the world. In their effort to achieve restful 'adjustment' to and 'integration' into unregenerate society they have lost their pilgrim character....They aren't lonely; but then neither are they saints."*

---

* A.W. Tozer, "The Saint Must Walk Alone," **Eternity**, August 1956, pp. 14, 11.

Followers sometimes fake their responses. They only seem to enter the leader's realm, even to the illusion of loneliness, but do not genuinely identify. They retain common pedestrian patterns in their lives. They may make claims of followership and show gestures of interest. Some announce their support, but nothing substantive is done. The leader, believing he has a treasure in them, discovers only "fool's gold." These persons may not know their true nature as far as the current purpose is related to them. Their attitudes only "feel" like the real thing. But they do not know enough about the circumstances, and their own interests are often at variance with the leader or leaders.

Alienation grows up between persons whose interests are at variance. There is commonly a spirit of alienation, a serious danger for society in war or economic depression. But it is at least mildly present in many interpersonal situations. Farmers may feel lonely and even alienated because they are prejudiced against by city voters. Urban citizens are offended at their country cousins who post pastures to prevent hunting or trespass. The wealthy are alienated from the poor; and the "have nots" from the "haves." This is meaningful perception for the understanding of "aloneness."

LEADERSHIP IMPOSES WEARINESS (Exodus 18:18)

Leaders soon learn they will not be rested if they do everything they ought to do, or are expected to do. It has been said that the world is run by tired men. This is not to say that their weariness is excessive. But leadership imposes physical and emotional tolls. Weariness is inevitable for leaders. It is some of the evidence of full-time leadership. It is a special weariness born of responsibility and creative effort, of being too much with other people, of inability to meet expectations, of never being free from duty.

Fatigue itself is a matter of study. It is commonly believed that the best way to overcome mental and emotional fatigue is to achieve personal success. But fatigue is not so simply understood. One may be confronted with *start-up fatigue*. Barely begun, the would-be leader perceives the problems he must overcome. He may not have the willpower to turn himself on to the job. Early grappling with issues must be made if success is to be gained. He puts it off. He may resign. Or the leader may have *performance fatigue*, in that he is not doing everything necessary to succeed, including getting along with others. Sooner or later adjustments must be made. He not only wants the right job but wants to do the job right. There is of course *natural fatigue*, the weariness of the body. The person who is fatigued must discern what kind of fatigue is being experienced. If physical, one needs rest and food; if mental, he needs time; if emotional, he needs some temporary change, like a vacation.

The issue of fatigue arises in the vignette between Moses and his father-in-law, Jethro. Visiting Moses during the early months of Israel's wilderness journey, Jethro returns Zipporah and her sons to Moses. The written account focuses more upon Moses and Jethro than the immediate family of Moses and Zipporah and their reunion. Moses, holding high regard for Jethro, recites the remarkable experience of the deliverance and movement of Israel. But Jethro is appalled at the volume of work falling to Moses in daily decision and judgment making.

Jethro states that Moses' work is not good, in that it will exhaust him, and exhaust the people as well. Undoubtedly Jethro meant that with only one person authorized to make decisions the people would have to wait too long for response. Delay would surely undermine confidence. In addition, many decisions would be unsatisfactory, made too quickly and without sufficient evidence or reflection.

Jethro does not promise Moses total relief, but advises that as primary leader Moses maintain the duty of approaching God, and fulfilling spiritual exercises. Then, with whatever time remains, Moses was to take on only the significant knotty problems that would, by their resolution, set precedent and policy for the people. Lesser officers could decide lesser issues.

Later, after years as leader of the people, Moses elects to make reference to this administrative decision, prompted by Jethro, as the special means God provided for the successful guidance of the people. He may have combined the counsel of Jethro with that of God to select a group of seventy elders. He credits the plan as special from God (Deut. 1:9-18). One wonders if Moses did not begin with the Jethro plan, gradually reassume heavier duties and was finally directed specifically by God to choose a sensible shared administration to meet all the needs of the people. In it is the essence of democracy.

No plan will end weariness in leaders who do what they ought to do. From time to time Moses complained about his weariness, about the excessive burden that God had given him in the people of Israel. Centuries later, writing to the Corinthians, the Apostle Paul complained, or at least noted, that he was often weary (2 Cor. 11:27). It is not something that leaders, ancient or modern, easily accept. Nearly all persons, leaders or followers, protest the requirement of weariness. Followers may quit, leaders should not.

We hope that we can do what we are supposed to do in life and still be rested. The combination is impossible for most situations. Leaders, and some of their followers, will not save causes on forty-hour work weeks. Those who reject weariness must reject leadership—perhaps also followership—in meaningful life experiences. The oft-weariness of the apostle Paul, coupled with jeopardy, hunger and cold, informs us about the apostle, but also tells us something about ourselves. What if he had, like so many of us, a neurotic fear of loneliness and weariness?

That person must be commended who bears weariness and refuses depression because of it. There is satisfaction in weariness that accomplishes its purpose. Rest, we hope, will follow. But true rest belongs not to the rested but to the weary.

Perhaps most of us evade opportunity because of its physical cost. Karl Olsson reminds his readers about their fear of tension and their desire for relaxation:

I read that a psychiatrist advises lying down on the floor as a way to release tension. When you start to feel taut, you are to plop on the floor at once, says this doctor. A bed won't do....All this would be fine if we could convince ourselves that the aim of faith is to relax us, to make us into innumerable potato sacks with the binding pulled out. But I think all this talk about relaxing is putting the cart before the horse. Of course it is bad to be overly tense; it is a sign of emotional illness. But how do we get that way? Certainly not by working too hard. We work "too hard" because we are tense and not vice versa. When we are truly free people, that is, people who through the mystery of grace are being released from the subtle pressure of guilt, anxiety and frustration, we work with great joy....*

No matter how magnificent the goal or scintillating the risk, many persons tire of their assignment. It is, in such cases, weariness of spirit that is most threatening, not weariness of body. Isaiah observed: "Thou art wearied in the greatness of thy way." That is to say, we are weary because our way is long, the journey is lengthy and tiring (Isa. 57:10).

We sometimes evade responsibility by blaming failure

---

* Karl A. Olsson, "Relax," **Covanent Weekly**, July 6, 1956, p. 12.

on institutions or other nonpersonal causes. Historians, like Arnold Toynbee, report that movements and nations get "tired" and stall in history. They often drop out of sight. Herbert Palmquist observed:

> It seems we are always chewing on something. Years ago it was the Interchurch World movement....Some people thought it was going to save the world; others were equally sure that it would damn the world. It did neither. Like MacArthur's "old soldier," it just faded away and most people don't even remember that it ever existed. Then there was the Oxford movement ....then there was the One-World idea... [and] that of the population explosion.*

None of the movements referred to by Palmquist fell merely from its own weight. They failed or weakened partly because the leaders and followers failed or weakened. Some critics believe democracy is losing because those who must believe in it in order for it to succeed have weakened their grasp. Russian communism, we are told by current analysts, has lost its idealism and cannot be compared to the communism of Lenin, nor even of Stalin, or Khruschev. If it has lost because the leaders are tired of the decades of trying to make communism work, they may fail. "They are weary because the journey is long." The phrase may be applied to circumstances and people, whether secular or sacred.

If we are tired because of our journey, the future is not to be admired. When Israel became weary in the greatness of her way, Phinehas' wife declared "Ichabod" (the glory has departed) over the life of the nation (1 Sam. 4:19-22). It was a departure partly brought on by lack of leadership from Eli and his sons. If the Lord departs from Israel, or from the Church, the leadership of both will

---

* Herbert E. Palmquist, "Let the Words of My Mouth Be Chaste," **The Covenant Companion**, May 20, 1960, p. 13.

change and followers will be different.

Informed leaders expect weariness, and they expect also to sustain their self-control. The gospel writers noted the weariness of Jesus, but He was always in control of Himself. He rested by Jacob's well, but took time to teach the Samaritan woman. He took His disciples away for rest and recuperation, but sublimated His own needs to minister to pursuing congregations. His exhaustion was apparent in His walk to the crucifixion site. H.G. Wells, in his *Outline of History*, stated that Jesus must have been weak, for He expired before the two malefactors died. Not only did Wells disregard the voluntary nature of Jesus' death, but the exhaustion from the lengthy trial, scourging, sleeplessness, and cross-bearing. To this we add the ministry preceding His suffering. The weariness of Jesus related in part to the rigors of leadership.

Weariness is in the nature of things and is therefore the lot of committed humankind. Steps must be taken to alleviate it. Even tired or weary animals retreat and rest. Plant life rests from growth. Apparently only man drives himself onward beyond his natural spiritual, social, mental, physical and emotional capacities. God rested after His creation, and He affords man days of rest. Even so, observing those days will not fully rest the leader.

LEADERSHIP IMPOSES ABANDON

There is nothing in Moses' experience in Midian, as we have it, that suggests he would possess the necessary characteristics to lead a million people out of slavery into freedom, through a wilderness to the gates of their own new country and nationhood. He had revealed his loyalty in the protection of a fellow Israelite, but his action led to loss of life for an Egyptian.

Moses was forced at forty years of age to flee Egypt to save his own life. Midian appears to have been a safe haven. Moses devoted his life in Midian to Jethro's business. His act of bravery, protecting Jethro's daughters in a just cause, gained their father's attention. Moses, employed by Jethro, ultimately married Zipporah, a daughter of his benefactor. Forty years after his Egyptian flight, he remained an employee of his father-in-law. The only creative observation for the period is that Moses turned aside to discover why a bush would burn without being consumed. At that point, God commanded Moses to go to Egypt and rescue Israel. After demurring and debating, Moses accepted and proceeded, clumsily at first, to become Israel's champion.

An abandon grew on Moses. Tentative during first gestures, he became stronger, less fearful for his own safety, more confident for God's will and way. He stood up to Pharaoh, counting more and more on the rightness of his cause, and the authority of his call. Later, in the wilderness, he stood up before all the people, to Aaron, and ultimately even to God. In all this we have a lesson.

What we have by way of freedom in the United States came to us neither by conservative nor liberal leaders exclusively. No matter what philosophy dominated, leaders took risks. The Pilgrims, the Puritans, the settlers to the westward took risks and they knew they did. Their abandon inspired others. The signers of the Declaration of Independence were men of abandon. They risked a great deal. They were not fearful of their future or "what course other men may take."

Church history is well populated by risk-takers. There would have been no Reformation without men like Martin Luther, John Hus, John Wycliffe, Count Zinzendorf. Their lives, even their deaths, inspire risk-takers in our era. In business we marvel at the abandon of Thomas Edison, Henry Ford, Henry J. Kaiser, and others. Kaiser sold steel to build a bridge in Spokane, Washington, while others were discussing the project. He built roads, knowing little about road building. Opportunity was just about all he cared about. He mastered shipbuilding with the goal to provide at least a liberty ship a day by the end of World War II. He did it. By 1960, Kaiser's empire was sufficiently large that in Oakland, California, two telephone exchanges, roughly equal in size, were constructed. One was for the city and the other was for Kaiser Industries. Kaiser built cars, aluminum plants, steel factories, and a score of other industries. He retired, moved to Hawaii, organized a whole living community, constructed a cement plant, and began a tiny new "empire" to close out his life.

There is abandon in Nathan before David, in Elijah on Carmel, in Moses before Pharaoh, in Paul before Agrippa, and in others before their friends or protagonists. By risking dynamic faith, they prevailed. Robert Louis Stevenson named overconcern with safety, security and prudence as the "dismal fungus." Leaders sometimes risk all of these. Workers or followers are far more interested in safety, security and highly predictable activity than leaders.

Leaders are, in formal situations, vulnerable to the loss of their jobs, to being brought down, to loss of income and power. They have few or no unions, no guarantees, no tenure. Most persons are unwilling for that threat of uncertainty. They are preoccupied with health and longer life, with regular income, limited responsibility, standard schedules and predictable outcomes. One wonders if the apostle Paul, as a patient, was a trial to Luke, the physician. Paul's work schedule, his poor diet, his exposure to nature's elements, his lack of rest—all violated appropriate medical recommendations. We might be critical of Paul. But Paul wrote supportively about his danger, and the challenge of untouched new lands. To him this was not egotistical reporting but evidence of leading forward to take opportunity. He was a risk-taker.

Is greater failure caused by excess of caution than by uncertain experimentation? How can we know? Perhaps we cannot know. Would we have left businesses as fishermen, farmers, tax-gatherers, to go with an itinerant preacher, One who left a small construction business to preach a new kingdom? Those fishermen were not unsuccessful in their work, they were not disgruntled with life or their families, but their abandon to the new call was an evidence of their potential for leadership. They did not play it safe. They were bold enough to change. They in turn became agents of world change.

LEADERSHIP IMPOSES VISION

Vision is several things, but an important element of vision that keeps one from becoming too visionary is the ability to see his place realistically in the vision. Can I see my place in the future? Or, at least, do I see the place I ought to hold in the future? It appears that those who have some clarity about themselves will, if sensible and practical, serve their followers best by having a fairly clear idea, although no certainty, of what they are about.

There is a sense in which we can make our future. What will it likely be if I take certain actions? And what will happen if I take these associates, instead of those, with me? For my own life, I have been fairly accurate about myself. Things have turned out just about the way I envisioned them. In earlier years my personal vision was not nearly as large as it should have been, so my life and leadership were less than would have been the case had I concluded an action plan before I did.

Then I began to take myself in greater earnestness and seriousness. My vision enlarged for myself, my family, the people with whom I worked, and the institutions of which I was a part. When appropriate strategies were tied to the vision, and the machinery set in motion, I discovered at first that the reality became larger than the vision. Where performance had once fallen short of my fantasies, now accomplishments, no matter how modest to others, ran ahead of my vision. And that differential—fantasy versus vision—may be a secret of failure and success, of happiness and disappointment.

Fantasy is based on dreams, wistfulness, even fiction. Fantasy is ghost smoke. There is no substance, no assurance to it. It is unreal in the way we make reference here. If a fantasy comes to pass, it is accidental, occurring so seldom in human experience that even gamblers would reject its odds.

Vision is much more. It is backed by faith. For me, that faith is in God as first Generator. But there are lesser faiths with meaningful dimension. Part of my vision is in the trustees of the institution I serve, the mentors who

---

FIGURE THREE

Vision vs. fantasy

Vision	Fantasy
Accomplishments often exceed vision.	Performance falls short of fantasy.
Backed by realistic faith (in God, in others, in self).	Based on dreams, wistfulness. Has no substance or assurance.
Plans are formulated to make vision come to pass.	If it comes to pass, it is by accident.
Leads to success, happiness.	Leads to failure, disappointment.

aided me in gaining my education, the family that stands by me. Unlike fantasy, this faith is based on factual material—what God is like, what my mentors are doing, what my family has done and may be expected to do. Then my own participation in my future is incorporated into the vision. Given the facts, I project what the future will be for me.

Projecting the future, based on knowledge, I begin the living. But I discover that I did not figure in everything. I must drop or add some activities. In the plan I may be able to fill in some gaps, and not fill others. Amendments follow. Dynamics shift as we knew they would. Additional solicitations of support, of various kinds, are made. Plans are revised to make the vision become reality. And like a jigsaw puzzle, when all pieces are available and in place according to their order, the vision becomes reality, having been constructed a bit at a time. So the vision is tempered, even changed by future realities. Vision, like all creative methodologies, must be flexible to amendments.

Vision is partly the ability of a person to see the conclusions toward which his ideas and activities tend. The Christian lacking appropriate values has lost his vision of who he is and what he is about, wrote the apostle Peter: "He is blind, *and cannot see afar off*, and hath forgotten that he was purged from his old sins" (2 Pet. 1:9).

What is ahead for us if we continue to do what we are now doing? A leader and his best followers ought to foresee something of what his policies will do in the course of time. This is basic to family leadership. What will my present conduct do in stimulating conduct in my children? Are my habits means for leading my children? We knew they were. So we set standards and kept them. Vision had something to do in our family with the choice of our language habits, with the banishment of liquor from our home, with the choice of entertainments, with the selection of book titles and topics of conversation. They were chosen or rejected, not primarily for their meaning for me, but because of their possible meaning for my family members. There is even this small self-denial in visionary leadership.

Vision is reliant upon hope. For those without hope the past pulls them magnetically, almost irresistibly. The future is too dimly lit for such people. They find enjoyment in closed memories. The past must push us, never pull us. Those looking too longingly to the past appear clumsy—as runners do when they look backward during a race. Our important business lies in front of us, near and far. If we do not do those things we ought to do, according C.S. Lewis, "We will find that we come to the end of life doing neither what we want to do nor what we ought to have done." If we do as we ought we will come to the end of life and discover we did what we really wanted to do.

Vision may be the beginning of evidence of leadership ability in a person. Dr. Warren Bennis, the eminent professor at the University of Southern California, begins with vision in his analysis of leaders and their ways. His concept of vision, and the full range of leadership characteristics is impressive, even though the factors he expounds have been reviewed by others as well. Bennis perceives five factors, repeating themselves in the scores of leaders he has interviewed: 1) Vision, 2) Creation, 3) Consistency, 4) Positiveness, and 5) Distancing.

By *vision* he means intentionality. Bennis believes leaders translate intention into reality. There is a kind of awareness about what they want. They perceive an outcome. At the full they do not waste time, either their own or that of others.

By *creation* he means that ideas become embodied in leaders. It is more than communication, although communication is included, in sharing that creation. There is a kind of excitement in making something new.

By *consistency* he means that leaders stay on course. They have a focus and keep it, even sharpen it. This gives them integrity. People know they can trust such leaders. Consistency creates trust.

By *positiveness* he means positive or affirmative self-regard. The ego is healthy, not active for itself. There is a fit between these leaders and the cause or institution they lead. This ego can identify strengths. These leaders are discerning. They know how to deploy themselves. They like to venture, and to feel a kind of glory in what they do.

By *distancing* he means that leaders lengthen the space between themselves and failure. They do not spend time explaining themselves to attackers. To answer attacks uses up time so they should not be dignified with answers except in special instances. Distancing helps keep leaders from diverting attention. Failing to distance self from failure may contribute to failure.

Vision eludes us. If it did not, we would not be wailing at forty years of age that we would do better if we had life to live over. There is time left for new things, for larger opportunities. We need not relive portions of our lives. We can now do, for many concerns, what we wish we had done earlier.

Myopia is our problem. We are nearsighted. We do things for now. That means we delay the right change in ourselves. We do not go with Pascal, who "bet" on God and the future. The wager is really vision, not a gamble. Faith evidence is too large for mere chance.

For those with hope, the past pushes them forward rather than pulls them backward. What is past provides foundation for the future. It took some time for Moses to understand the principle of the foundation of history. Loath to lead at first, then willing, Moses at length arrived at the disillusionment stage. If he could only be free of this massive duty. He yearned to get these thankless people off his back. But disillusionments provide real life. Similar lows, fitting circumstances, are inevitable for leaders who remain at their tasks.

During the elapse of time, Moses began to identify more fully with the whole venture. Vision became stronger and gave fresh inspiration. Particular discouragements and separate defeats no longer were permitted to distort the meaning of his total objective. Moses became the complete leader. The trinity of leadership futures broke through: vision, integrity, and patience.

This dedication to completion is made at a crossroads in Moses' life. Israel, having failed, is sufficiently irritating that God has reason to dissolve the tribes and abandon His plan to set them up as His people. In the dissolution, their leader could become the father of the new people of God. Instead of Israelites, the Mosesites would found a nation. Moses is faced with the choice of leadership to Israel or patriarchy to his own issue. Which road will he take? Should he stand up to God and affirm his purpose, or should he acquiesce and change that purpose? Either possibility has threat and promise in it.

In this choice Moses shows himself the leader, not the founder of a nation. The people sinned in worshipping the golden calf. Even Aaron, like Eli later, failed in leadership. In the tale, it appears that the whole plan is collapsing, perhaps it has collapsed. The people were "out of control" (Ex. 32:25). Aaron had let it happen, partly out of his own disgust. The people would become a derision to their enemies, unless the situation were recovered.

Moses became his own spokesman. He moved beyond Aaron, upon whom he had so fully counted and from whom failure generated. He called for followers. All of

Levi turned to him. Moses, with the Levites, forcefully put down, in blood, those violating the Lord's way. Moses then called for trust from survivors that he would find atonement. He sought the answer. The people waited and Moses talked with God. In the exchange God proposed to destroy Israel and make Moses a nation. But Moses had promised the people a search for forgiveness, not an alternate plan.

Moses refused God's offer, putting himself at great risk. He insisted on forgiveness. If God will not forgive the people, Moses said, then also "blot me out from thy book which thou hast written" (Ex. 32:32). It was a high point in leadership for Moses. He had traveled this far with Israel, and he would not be satisfied until God's plan was fulfilled according to the original vision.

Formerly Moses was a figure of acceptance to the people, but he complained about his assignment in privacy with God. With years behind him in the wilderness, he complained to the people about their conduct but defended them effectively before God. The circle of understanding was complete. From this point he could lead and enjoy his assignment. The full cost of his ministry was paid.

Those who have hope will know legitimate optimism, will know that all things work together for good to those who love God. In the end, Moses revealed that mature development. The evidence is strong and emerges to us on the day of Moses' greatest personal disappointment. High on the mountain of Abarim, Moses views the landscape of Canaan. To go into that promised land would fulfill forty years of arduous labor in leadership. But because Moses had challenged God's leadership at the waters of Meribah at Kadesh, Moses would not be permitted to enter the land. He would die before the goal was reached.

What would be our response to so great

disappointment? We respond bitterly to lesser denials. We lose a privilege, an opportunity, a goal, and we complain. On occasion we pay a higher price in our reaction than in our constructive action. A man set his heart on acquisition of a piece of property. With that site he would do marvelous things. But God refused him through the decisions of men. For a short period he fell apart. Dismay took him. He temporarily lost his natural spirit. Practical decision making eluded him. His ability to role model for his people declined somewhat. He lost his leadership position in that place because of his Kadesh. He was forced to start over again in another place. By the grace of God, and a new vision tailored to his situation, he did well. He might have saved the first one with better vision. He needed to know more about paying the price of risk-taking, for there is a price, whether success or failure follows the action.

What did Moses do? He requested from God a new leader to see the work through to the end: "May the Lord...appoint a man over the congregation, who will go out and come in before them, and who will lead them out and bring them in, that the congregation of the Lord may not be like sheep which have no shepherd" (Num. 27:16-17).

It followed that Moses commissioned Joshua with charge and the laying on of hands before the people. Eleazar, the high priest after Aaron's death, dedicated Joshua to leadership before God. That began another story of leadership with its personal and public advancement, defeat, planning, amendment, success and history.

What did Moses leave us by way of information about ourselves and leadership? He teaches us that leadership can be learned, can be improved, can be selfless. Like Moses, we can move upward in leadership from one plateau to another. On those higher plateaus situations appear in different perspective. We must be willing to be evaluated, able to win or lose, and prepared to make sacrifices. Each is difficult for us. We may not pay the price. It is easier to drift than lead. It is easier to ride than push, to accept only modest accomplishment than risk blame. Moses' life of leadership evidences the imposition of loneliness, weariness, abandon and vision carried by a leader—at least carried by God's leader.

Does Moses have more to teach about leadership? Certainly he does, and we turn to him for more, that we may know better how to lead.

—3—

The Preliminary of Leadership
RELATIONSHIPS

And Moses said unto Hobab, the son of Reuel the Midianite, Moses' father in law, We are journeying unto the place of which the Lord said, I will give it you: come thou with us, and we will do thee good: for the Lord hath spoken good concerning Israel.

And he said unto him, I will not go; but I will depart to mine own land, and to my kindred.

And he said, Leave us not, I pray thee; forasmuch as thou knowest how we are to encamp in the wilderness, and thou mayest be to us instead of eyes.

And it shall be, if thou go with us, yea it shall be, that what goodness the Lord shall do unto us, the same will we do unto thee.

And they departed from the mount of the Lord three days' journey: and the ark of the covenant of the Lord went before them in the three days' journey, to search out a resting place for them.

And the cloud of the Lord was upon them by day, when they went out of the camp.

—Numbers 10:28-34

The text recites part of an experience between Moses and his brother-in-law, Hobab. Hobab, like his father, Jethro, was a man of integrity and wisdom. When he made an appeal to Hobab, Moses seems not yet to have learned all he needed to know about the remarkable Jethro (Reuel) family. But Moses had learned enough not to lose on first try and first strategy. He knew to probe for effective motivation.

Moses begins by inviting Hobab to trek with Israel. Moses needs Hobab to guide the nation over the best trails. This is country known to Jethro's family. Perhaps, too, Moses likes Hobab and welcomes the companionship of so fine a fellow. Moses' strategy is to appeal to Hobab's self-interest: "Come with us and we will do thee good." By joining the entourage Hobab will have honor, privilege, and other benefits. To Moses' surprise, Hobab demurs, rejects the offer, and prepares to return home.

Perceptively, Moses shifts strategy at once, a sign of his growing leadership effectiveness. Hobab is told, in straightforward language, that he is needed. He can be guide to the people, save time, avoid battle with hostile or fearful tribes, and thus serve both God and Israel. With that motivational appeal, Hobab joins the retinue.

It is likely that Hobab shuttled back and forth between his home grounds and Israel's encampment. Israel was not always on the move. Encampments would remain for months, even years, at a time. Hobab's expertise would not be needed for long periods, so the man could go where he wished and where he perceived himself to be most productive.

Hobab must have been a man of diplomacy. He could direct a million people to move from one wilderness living site to another. The problems could have become insurmountable, and they certainly would have been had the people not been skillfully mobilized. Orderly movement of material and people, with problems of communication and ordinance, could have become virtually impossible to resolve. Hobab kept these factors manageable. He could work well with people. He did what he did better than Moses could do it, but it took a leader like Moses to get a leader like Hobab to do it for Israel. That is a large part of leadership: finding and employing competent people, who can work with other people.

When an individual works well with others, he is tactful. A survey of 80,000 employees in 76 companies or corporations sought to discover why as candidates for promotions they were turned down. Primary cause was lack of tact. Slightly more than three out of four (76.5%) persons were turned down because they were believed to be unable to get along with people. We might have guessed their rejection was because of ignorance about the jobs they were hoping to get. But they failed to advance because of a lack of knowledge about people or an unwillingness to make personal adjustments required in working with people.*

To become a consistent leader, one must know something about himself, where he is going in life, and that he is willing to stay at his task. He should ask himself: "What kind of leader do I wish to become? In what way does that differ from what I am now?" He must also ask: "What more do I need to know about myself?"

---

* **Human Relations**, The Stevens-Davis Company, Chicago, Illinois, April 20, 1955, p. 2.

A very large part of the answer to those questions is found in understanding his relationships with people.

LEADERSHIP MEANS GETTING
ALONG WITH PEOPLE FOR A PURPOSE

Leaders know they need people. They need followers, to be sure, but they need followers who are leaders also. Moses discovered early enough that he could not do everything. He needed help in several departments of administration. When Hobab filled the role of guide, Moses became a more effective leader. We find other follower-leaders in the Israel sojourn. When they succeeded, Moses seemed to succeed. When they failed, Moses seemed to fail. This pattern can be readily seen in the ebb and flow of Aaron's leadership as high priest. Even the influence of Miriam, Moses' sister, had something to do with several events and with the public perceptions of her brother.

A leader needs his or her mate, needs stewards, workers, friends, relatives, neighbors to help in the cause, to take over projects, to practice loyalty, procedures and techniques to assure success for the leader and his proper purposes. As noted earlier, we learned that in leadership fields the best way to overcome professional fatigue is to perceive success in what one is doing. Success requires, in most instances, effective cooperation between persons. To keep subordinates at the task, the leader must give them a perception of success. Cooperation dies quickly in losing causes.

If the leader cannot get along with people in a democratic society he will likely lose his place. He may then wish he had never made first rank, for to decline in status is too great disappointment. He loses face. If a project fails the leader is usually expected to take responsibility for events. Appointments were his, and he designed or accepted strategies. He would have been honored in the event of success, so he must accept some ignominy for failure. (In much of the world failure is accompanied by some ignominy. Unfortunately, in a highly competitive society, there is ignominy in just about anything less than first place.)

Cause for failure, then, may be found in a leader's inability to get along with people. Joseph, eldest of Rachel's sons to Jacob, is perceived by youthful Sunday school children to be the faultless victim of his jealous brothers. No one can justify the conduct of the brothers in kidnapping and selling Joseph into slavery. But there is reason to believe that young Joseph was something of a snip. Not only was he the obvious favorite of his father, but he wore a magnificent jacket of many colors, a nonverbal emblem parading his status. The conduct of the father and favorite son was not well directed to lead older sons into ideal attitudes and responses. To gain so wide support among so many brothers for the deed of kidnapping and selling their brother to a wandering band, suggests that something in the family attitudes of father Jacob and son Joseph were less than satisfactory.

A prospective leader may not have a chronic problem in getting along with people—but he can create periodic episodes nonetheless. If the problem were chronic he would not likely make an effective leader. But virtually all leaders suffer periodic clashes with others. Some conflict is in the nature of things. Moses lost the people on occasion. So did David. When David fled from the palace during Absalom's attempt to usurp the throne, he must have wondered where he was in error. How could the formerly loyal citizens turn on him? How could they be persuaded by the oily diplomacy of Absalom? After David's restoration the people rightfully must have felt embarrassment. How could they have forsaken their king for the young and handsome opportunist?

We need to be reminded that leadership, even excellent

leadership, may not succeed. Success is not the ultimate measure of a leader. Jesus was a leader. Everyone knew that He was. He was crucified, and His followers were scattered. Ultimate success of Jesus' leadership, a leadership that has held for nearly two thousand years, came after His death and resurrection. Even His enemies knew Jesus was a leader during the months of His ministry. His announcements related, at the beginning of His ministry, to His leadership. His call to disciples was a call to follow Him. We are told that people followed Him gladly. Following Him was a major matter in His teaching, so He acclaimed Himself a leader. His leadership was and is necessary to His ministry and mission.

Jesus experienced, as all leaders experience, the periodic loss of followers. On occasion the disciples were partly lost in their faultfinding, their pride, their push for status, their concern about reward. By the end of Jesus' ordeal and death they had fled. It appeared, even to His friends, that He had failed. The physician had not healed himself. After the resurrection the scattered disciples were reconstituted. But the later success does not deny the quality and rightness of Jesus' leadership before the resurrection. Failure was in followership.

Many followers of Jesus at the time were even less certain than the first disciples. The larger bodies (the 70 and the 120) held different views of their commitment to Jesus and His leadership. Various writers believe that some who shouted, "Hosannah," on the triumphal entry, shouted, "Crucify Him," less than a week later. We speculate further that many who said, "Crucify Him," also later returned to follow Jesus.

Students of leadership would prefer to discuss effectiveness or ineffectiveness rather than success or failure. The point here is that leadership is not to be measured by common ideas of success, but through achievement relative to announced purposes. The leader makes clear where he is going. If he misses his goal, the failure may be primarily in the followers, or in timing for the cause in history, or something else. Robert E. Lee was a great leader in a losing cause. Evaluation is concerned in part in finding out if the leader and the followers function well. On occasion a mediocre leader succeeds because of effective followers. They make him "look good."

Even so, an effective leader should know himself: his tolerances, his tact with people, and his personality adaptability to the cause. Seldom can one make it on his own. Individualism, achieving by one's own efforts, is not leadership. Leadership always implies that someone is following.

At times the leader feels alone, as noted earlier, and sometimes he is alone or feels as though he is. But he cannot always be alone. Even David, going out alone against Goliath, needed backup from the army of Israel to engage the Philistine army. A slingshot and an exotic plan to be rid of a massive soldier will not fell an army. David, having proved himself a brave and resourceful man, needed the backing of other men to accomplish victory. Hard work and effective leadership followed the death of Goliath.

An important evidence of leadership is knowledge about people's needs. Abraham Maslow, the eminent psychologist, argued that effective managers should know and use the "hierarchy of human needs." The list often appears in materials for leadership training. Although they are sometimes misconstrued or distorted, those needs are important. Jerry Chaplin proposed that Jesus used them, and we find them in Moses' manner of governance.

1. Physical needs were met by Moses in the design for manna as daily bread. Jesus fed the five thousand and enhanced His ministry through appeals to the physical well-being of people. Healing was important in the public acceptance of Jesus.

2. Security needs were met by Moses in the pillar of fire by night and the cloud by day. Jesus calmed the sea when His disciples were fearful. The disciples hoped for security in anticipating that Jesus would become governor or king in Israel.

3. Social needs were met by Moses in providing a rest day in seven, musicians and priests, religion with its accoutrements, and the like. Jesus went to a wedding feast and began His public ministry there. It appears that He often introduced ideas, even discourses, at meals. The ''last supper'' is significant example. He appears to have taught during and following breakfasts. Jesus was a social person and used social contexts favorably in His discourses.

4. Self-esteem needs were met by Moses in relating Israel to God as His special people. Israel later distorted the meaning by developing a religious racial pride partly denigrating other races. Jesus particularized the idea in such promises as providing thrones for the disciples in

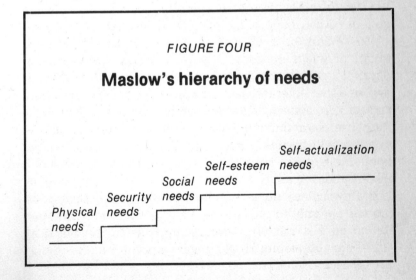

FIGURE FOUR

Maslow's hierarchy of needs

Physical needs

Security needs

Social needs

Self-esteem needs

Self-actualization needs

His kingdom. The mother of the sons of Zebedee requested special consideration for the placement of thrones for her sons. Jesus must have smiled in response, for, as He pointed out, heaven is not like earth, therefore His people needed a different view of reward and bliss. Even so, Jesus cast his ideas for human perception.

5. Self-actualization needs were met by Moses in giving the people work to do. Jesus also gave work to His followers, attaching high rewards and rights to the accomplishment of His purposes. Work is a major theme in the Bible, and the promise of human/spiritual resources to do the work is also major. (During the twentieth century, work has been given too little attention in the popular theology of the Church.)

It is a truism that when all needs are met there is a general sense of well-being among satisfied people. Those who wish to lead seek that general well-being for their followers, at least in the areas over which they exert influence.

LEADERSHIP MEANS PERSUADING PEOPLE TO DO WHAT THEY OUGHT TO DO

Effective leaders commonly need to know the elements of persuasion. Ethical persuasive practice differentiates leaders from autocrats or authoritarians. It is persuasion, an appeal to logical reason and emotional motivation, that characterizes a democratic leader, at least in the sense we wish to use leadership here. Leaders will, when occasion demands, give an order. But order giving is not the great evidence of a leader. Many orders are issued by persons who are not, and never will be, leaders. Order giving, at one time or another, is done by nearly everyone. It is more the function of current status (boss to worker, parent to child) than anything else.

Persuasion is ethical when rightfully practiced. Ethical

leadership utilizes that persuasion. The Scriptures make major issue of persuasion. It is traceable as a leading factor in the work of judges, kings, prophets, disciples, and Jesus. Rhetoric was vital to them. It was not "mere" rhetoric, or "empty" rhetoric, but the gospel freighted through the principles and practices of ethical persuasion. In the biblical perception the gospel is dependent upon persuasion. The apostle Paul wrote: "Knowing therefore the terror of the Lord, we persuade men" (2 Cor. 5:11). In his first letter to the Corinthians the apostle implied a large theory of sacred rhetoric. Several centuries later Augustine authored the first treatise on sacred rhetoric that began a necessary and honorable tradition in "homiletics."

Moses opened his persuasive effort to Hobab by promising him personal benefits. The offer was not unethical, but it was ineffective with Hobab. It was a failing effort. A leading principle in persuasion, as stated by Aristotle, is to use all appropriate available means to accomplish ethical purposes. By shifting his appeal from self-interest to service for others, Moses succeeded. He shifted motivations from self-esteem to self-actualization and won his purpose with Hobab. Another person than Hobab might well have responded to self-esteem. Hobab was sufficiently fulfilled and self-confident without the public acclaim of the tribes. He was far enough along to serve without excessive honors. A willingness to serve without great reward is one sign of a high achieving leader.

For many persons the first appeal would have worked. Self-interest might be their first or dominant motivation. Moses needed an experienced guide. If he could get one through self-interest he would make that appeal. There is no reason to believe that Hobab would have been an inferior guide if he had joined the company for lesser reason than he did. In any event, Hobab shows himself a high-principled man in the context. He responded to selfless motivations, to commitment for doing good. Perhaps he could well afford, in the prosperity of his own business, to disregard any personal benefit Moses might provide for him.

Hobab would not respond to the "enlightened self-interest" type of argument. Moses quickly discovered in Hobab's response and attitude that he had taken the wrong track to accomplish his purposes. He had not analyzed his man well enough. Like a well-informed persuader, insightful in the one-to-one situation, Moses shifted his appeal. Would Hobab come along with the people because he could do them good? Yes, he could do that. Apparently he did it.

Hobab, like many men and women we have known, was a giver. Perhaps he was a philanthropist. One takes a different tack in persuasion to gain response from a giver than a receiver. And this observation is not to denigrate receivers. Receivers are well-addressed in the hierarchical needs described by Maslow. What happens when they no longer wish for more than they have, no more than they can provide for themselves? Even with motivational shifting on their own, they wish to be a part of the passing parade. A new set of motivations or special uses of traditional ones begins to work in them.

Those who work with true philanthropists know that a different leadership is called for in working with them than with many others. Goals, means, accomplishment, accountability, targets, are main matters. Profits, honor, power and the like are relatively unimportant to the purist benefactor. He is more interested in results related to his ideals, and less interested in personal honors. He often doubts the sincerity of those honors anyway.

Persuasion survives from among ancient arts. Persuasion (rhetoric) was a major influence, perhaps the major influence in the human behavior of the most influential people during the golden ages of Greece and

Rome. A leader had to be something of an orator, a person who could defend himself or advocate a cause in a public forum. Rhetoricians (theorists) were highly influential, especially in the education of young men. They wrote about speech and/or taught youths how to speak well. Leaders then, leaders now, required and require persuasive talents. Students in the field find many similarities between the use of persuasion in ancient times with the use of it in modern life to accomplish leadership.

Three sweeping perceptions are basic to rhetoric: ethos, pathos and logos. *Ethos*, wrote Aristotle, is "the power of persuasion which lies within the man himself." By that he meant that the individual persuader should be, in his person, a driving force in his persuasion. The persuader is so highly regarded in his reputation, his accomplishments, his integrity, that people feel compelled to believe him and follow his proposal, his leadership. Hobab was likely impressed by the quality and power of the man Moses. He would find it difficult to refuse Moses' request. The people saw something special in Moses, who firmly related his purpose to God's will. They would do for Moses what they might not do even for Aaron, or some other leader. And Aaron's ethos would be persuasive, but it would not be as great as Moses'.

Certainly Jesus developed ethos that became so significant Roman and Jewish leaders had to contend with it, and neutralize it with the people, to accomplish their purposes to destroy Him. In the early apostolic church Peter held high ethos (Acts 8:14). Later, the apostle Paul won similar acceptance. The persuasive ability of the men related, in part, to their ethos. And their ethos partly related to their special relationship with Jesus.

In our time we are also impressed by the presence of men and women who have earned ethos. We are more pliant to their proposals, and permit them to lead.

Sometimes we are compelled by them.

Pathos is appeal to emotion, uniting emotional fire with truth. People must feel inclination if they are to act. Moses knew that people tend to do what they want to do. Because neither Israel nor the Egyptians would automatically respond to him, he would need a forceful speaker to gain attention and position. He was not (as yet) effective in his own public speech (Ex. 4:10-16). Aaron filled the vacuum. But because rhetorical skills can be taught and learned, Moses ultimately learned those principles for himself and applied them skillfully during later wilderness years.

Logos is logical argumentation, providing a base of intellectual integrity for the persuader and confidence in what he is doing and saying. In this is the meaning, the reasoning, the evidence for what followers ought to believe and do. Without the support of sound argument and evidence, ethos and pathos are without substance. What the leader says and does, if it violates truth and ethics, will ultimately cost him everything in ethos and pathos. This is well illustrated in the careers of Senator Joseph McCarthy in the 1950s and President Richard Nixon in the 1970s in American life.

LEADERSHIP MEANS
SHARING THE GLORY WITH THE PEOPLE

Wise leaders know that their appreciation for support groups is vital for continued effectiveness. In adequate ways, a sensitive leader honors those who serve under him. He must believe that those who aided him did more than he can account for in himself. Not all contributions are observed, but he wishes they were. He assumes there are important influences he cannot see and evaluate. If what he does know is positive, he should extend his generosity, assuming unknown contributions.

The Scriptures, by their very nature, are sometimes agonizingly limited in narrative. For example, the information available about Hobab is short in text, but highly commends the man. How did Moses show appreciation during the years that Hobab served? Did he commend him in the presence of other leaders, perhaps the congregation? Did he credit him where credit was due? Likely. In our terms: Did Moses hold a dinner for him (manna dishes, of course)? Did he give Hobab a special citation? Leaders, ancient and modern, have found ways of expressing appreciation for service in others. It is not easy to do, especially when contributions vary as widely as they do.

Some associates require more stroking than others. Many persons do not wish "to be made over." They do what they do and find honor, even gestures of appreciation, to be embarrassing. They make it clear that they wish anonymity. If their participation is not so treated, they withdraw and find a new arena for leadership and service. Those who make the greatest contributions are often the ones who wish the least attention. A leader has to discover and adjust to this and other ranges in human preferences.

A leader can do almost anything he wants to do, within reason, if he is untroubled about who gets the credit. Because some require more of this or that honor is not to presume they are weaker or more prideful than others. Their nurturing, conditioning, and general approach to life may require larger volumes of psychic rewards than their colleagues. The leader adjusts accordingly to re-assure his co-workers. A test of leader's confidence is the ability he has to "give away" his own credits to associates.

How may a leader remain alert to the importance of distributing honor? Perhaps leaders will remember how they wished for recognition when they were followers. A leader is sometimes a follower, and may perceive the needs of others in ego-satisfaction when he is. The principle applies in common family experiences. In marriage, issues of leadership telescope. She is a wise and confident mother/wife who can tolerate hearing her husband praised for her work, especially in running the household and nurturing the children. He is a wise husband who honors his wife with genuine compliments for the work and care she gives.

In labor-management negotiations discussion turns to issues of psychic income as well as monetary. Workers imply and sometimes argue that they hope for recognition, appreciation, respect, titles or the like. In 1981, during negotiations between the air traffic controllers and the government, their employer, selected controllers were interviewed relative to their demands and aspirations. Although increased salaries and reduced working hours were main matters, some controllers were interested in finding ways to honor their fellow workers when a particularly effective job was done. Because they were blamed for errors they committed, affecting aircraft safety, could something be done to praise them as readily when, by their skills alone, a mid-air collision or other catastrophe was avoided? (Later, in 1983, it was alleged that fired controllers had, on occasion, deliberately violated their trust by "creating" incidents in the air.)

Apparently forms of psychic income cannot easily be legislated in labor contracts. But more can be done to honor people for what they do. As a matter of policy, leaders can and do include recognition of their people in their techniques for carrying through purposes.

Even so, leaders know that recognition is not fully equitable. Followers commonly fault their leaders. Honors they presume to be due them may not be generated for the leader. Although they fault the leader, he cannot fault them. They interpret his criticism as disloyal to them. They commonly withdraw.

Insightful leaders must not be unduly depressed by the harshness they experience. Followers will sometimes unfairly attribute to them wrong motives, wrong views, even wrong conduct. In his writing, the eminent United States senator from Oregon, Mark Hatfield, a Christian gentleman, wrote about his great disappointment at scurrilous accusations against leaders, accusations made by men and women affirming themselves to be Christians. He hoped for objectivity and better analysis than he received.*

Among biblical leaders there appear both praise and rebuke. Jesus defended the disciples, but He also rebuked them. The first, praise, was done openly or in special ways. The second seems to have been done, for the most part, in private exchange. There might have been some public situations even if veiled. Jesus was stern with the disciples on their attempt to prevent mothers and children from reaching Him.

The leader may learn much about his own response from that of Jesus. Jesus gave appropriate explanations, even asked questions to guide conversations through. Sometimes they were well received and sometimes they were not. Concluding on occasion that no good would be served by His response, he fell silent. He refused to answer or debate when no benefit would accrue, or He was not seeking benefit. Would a defense on His part at His trial have turned the results?

Most of what is discussed in this chapter is related to what is called *tact*, referred to earlier. Tact is required because people differ from one another. What one needs or appreciates, another does not. A leader sifts through various factors for differences to serve purposes. One has

---

* Mark Hatfield, **Between a Rock and a Hard Place**, (Waco, Texas: Word Books, 1976), p. 13ff.
——————, **Conflict and Conscience** (Waco, Texas: Word Books, 1971), p. 21ff.

tact when he goes beyond his own perceptions of what he needs for accomplishment, to the insights and needs of others, and accepts those views to help guide him in responses.

How an idea or action is communicated may determine its acceptance. For myself, I like straightforward language with few euphemisms. When a man dies, I prefer to report he died. Family members may hope that matters will be softened for them. We find various means to pad realities that discomfort us. For some it is better to report that he "passed away," that he has "gone," or even "gone to be with the Lord." What is the best way to express an idea? The best way is that which serves others effectively, that accomplishes the purpose while generating the most congenial feeling. Political leaders are careful students of the pattern.

So a leader delays, when he must, to accommodate his people. He speeds up when they are ready to act. He explains, repeating when necessary, to accomplish goals. He is aware that even though he knows what is to be done, followers may find the course somewhat complicated to understand. He may recap the case several times. He does so with patience because he is a leader.

As a leader he can cope with disappointment, although he prefers victory. He can start, and stop, then start and stop, and start again. He knows that losing part is not losing all. A leader believes that the matter will emerge and end successfully. At least it will play out. The world, for such a person, will not end with this venture. There are new opportunities to be taken, and he will not terminate interest because either failure or victory has followed his last effort.

—4—

The Profession of Leadership
EVALUATION

Beloved, believe not every spirit, but try the spirits whether they are of God: because many false prophets are gone out into the world.

Hereby know ye the Spirit of God: Every spirit that confesseth that Jesus Christ is come in the flesh is of God:

And every spirit that confesseth not that Jesus Christ is come in the flesh is not of God: and this is that spirit of antichrist, whereof ye have heard that it should come; and even now already it is in the world.

Ye are of God, little children, and have overcome them: because greater is he that is in you, than he that is in the world.

They are of the world: therefore speak they of the world, and the world heareth them.

We are of God: he that knoweth God heareth us; he that is not of God heareth not us. Hereby know we the spirit of truth, and the spirit of error.

Beloved, let us love one another: for love is of God; and every one that loveth is born of God, and knoweth God.

He that loveth not knoweth not God; for God is love.

—1 John 4:1-8

The question is raised from time to time: "Can loving Christians be effective leaders?" It is a proper question for management and administration anywhere, either for secular or sacred institutions. The argument commonly raises the point whether sensitive Christians can be tough enough to do what must be done to accomplish leadership goals in difficult and comprehensive situations. Several persons who have worked under my administration, persons who formerly were employed by leading corporations, have expressed doubts about the will or talent of Christian leaders to make hard decisions and hold to them. For example, they felt that terminations of personnel should be more readily done by Christian administrations than is usually the case. Christian employers may be less willing than secular to fire workers. If true, this may be a virtue for Christian employers. But it may be that smaller corporations, managed by any persons, are less likely to terminate employees than large ones. Dynamics vary between large and small companies.

Some evaluators state that Christian employers are less likely to guarantee longevity of jobs than non-Christian. This ambivalence among observers about religious and secular employers extends into other areas. For example, few Christian organizations are taken to court for their personnel policies. This may well be due to the reluctance of most Christians to carry issues through litigation against spiritual brothers. Having worked for both

Christian and non-Christian employers, I feel that both have done well and both poorly all along the line in implementation of their duties and leadership. Circumstances and leaders vary in both contexts. It is not likely that systematic comparisons have been made between secular and religious businesses.

During the history of nations, Christian government leaders (presidents, kings, governors) seem neither to have performed more nor less effectively than non-Christian leaders. Following wars, Christian generals of armies often receive high praise. On occasion some of them have been reduced as heroes because of their activities and monumental egos. Similar ego patterns hold for non-Christian generals. Presidents and kings holding different religious persuasions receive mixed reports. Cromwell did not become a superior leader for England. The several presidents of the United States who are acknowledged to be genuinely Christian seem not to have displayed unusual talent as leaders. They followed mainline patterns historians chart for presidential performances. Except for personal modeling (an important factor), the talent for decision making and inspiration appears to level out throughout historical periods.

The reason for the choice of the text (1 John 4:1-8) introducing this chapter is twofold. One is that evaluation, trying a case, is necessary if we are to find assurance in a course of action. The second is that evaluation may be done in love. It can and ought to be acceptable as humane conduct. But it must be done to guarantee as much as possible the truth, progress and expectation in any venture.

There are "criticisms" that fail to qualify as evaluation. Gossip, vituperation, rumor, fabrication are almost always negative and damaging. Basic to evaluation is objectivity and deep desire to improve persons and situations for purposeful futures. Affirmative and constructive evaluation is designed, or should be, to solve problems.

The purpose of evaluation is to ascertain the results of any activity. Progress, or lack of it, is charted. New methods and activities are projected from the evaluation results.

LEADERS MAY EVALUATE
WHEN THEY HAVE COMPASSION

A leader tends to improve his administration by evaluating what he as well as others have done, and with what resources, relative to current concerns. What has happened: what will happen? From such evaluation he will adjust his plans, personnel, approaches, time frames, materials and other factors for future action. The choice of instruments used for evaluation has much to do with the reliability of the evaluation. High quality evaluation is made in an objective manner, but objectivity requires softening through the efforts of compassionate evaluators. The method should, if possible, avoid hurting people, or reduce hurt to minimal levels. The purpose is to get the evaluation accepted and recommended changes adopted.

When evaluators fail in compassion, they reveal themselves in characteristic conduct. They evaluate through their feelings, which is flimsy evaluation. Questions are cast in one-sided or judgmental ways, implying their own answers. Language often exposes prejudicial attitudes. The language used and the way it is used reveal the personal orientation of the leader. An autocratic, sometimes insensitive, boss may use absolutes such as "never" and "always" in making statements about worker conduct. But the worker only sometimes fails, so to say "always" misrepresents him. He is generally on time, so he is misrepresented when reported that he is "never" on the job at the assigned hour. What is the actual record of attendance?

Even selection of evidence reveals levels of good or ill will. Out of the prejudicial approach comes innuendo, even venomous talk. We expect right spirit and sound intellect in analysts, but we may not get either. Often evaluation is lost because those who try to lead do not know how to critique problems. Perhaps evaluation is for them the childish faultfinding they learned in elementary and high school. One of our daughters was deeply offended by the "slam books" of her high school days. Several pseudo-sophisticated girls developed the idea that their school yearbooks should become "slam books."

FIGURE FIVE

Compassionate vs. uncompassionate evaluation

Compassionate	Uncompassionate
Improves	Degrades
Analysis is objective	Analysis is based on feelings
There is reluctance to criticize	Questions are cast in judgmental ways
One evaluated is allowed to participate in critique	Language exposes prejudicial attitudes
Creative evaluative techniques are sought	Evidence is selected in prejudicial ways

Student procedure was to write something critical or negative about each class member, next to that person's photograph. Remarks were unkind, even venomous. One young student had a book filled with negative remarks made by classmates about other classmates. She requested slams for classmates from our daughter. One wonders what attitudes will characterize that student in adult life. The idea totally repulsed our daughter. Rightly so.

Just because there are persons acting in unkind ways, making scurrilous and ugly statements about us or others, we should not be unwilling to be evaluated. Evaluation is as different from gossip and "slam" conversation as prostitution is from marriage intimacy. There is a canyon of difference between picking on people and helping them through evaluative techniques. One degrades and the other improves.

Compassionate evaluation is observed in characteristic conduct. There ought to be genuine reluctance to communicate even necessary critique. When a leader must evaluate his people, their part in programs and methods, he tries to show that he is loath to do anything causing emotional pain to anyone. He may wish to talk privately with a person, may even ask the one to be evaluated what is the best way to do what he feels must be done.

In some way human caring must shine through. The person receiving the evaluation may not sense that faithful concern at first, but he will, in time. Even a child reacting to parental review of his conduct will, after first defensive reactions, recognize the love and concern of his parents for his welfare. One of my sons responded to such a review at one time, and when later asked by a neighbor how he felt about his father's remarks, the lad said, "If I didn't need it I wouldn't get it. Dad loves me."

Perhaps we can find creative ways to evaluate our lives

and circumstances, as well as those who look to us for leadership. Many persons have a gift for making their points. They have at least partial recognition of both the social problem, or whatever the large issue may be, and the human concern or sensitivity. The late Malvina Reynolds was a popular member of the San Francisco Bay area community of California. Driving the freeway, she observed the row houses in San Francisco and Daly City. She felt there was something wrong with cramped housing, so wrote a song, "Little Boxes," that hit the top of popularity charts. She made her points quietly, but she made them. She sang what she felt she had to say. And there was evaluation in it. People were forced to consider the issues set in such dramatic form. Later studies were designed to discover if Reynolds's "ticky-tacky" houses dehumanized their inhabitants. It was found that the citizens were happier about their circumstances than Malvina Reynolds believed them to be.

Compassion and love should hold, even when matters are miscast or misunderstood. Surely we will, on occasion, be misunderstood. I once knew a doctor who, in presenting an evaluation of a woman's health to the woman, told her she had a severe cancer that needed immediate attention. She "refused" to accept the diagnosis. The woman, offended at the physician, began scurrilous gossip about his competency as a doctor. She died of cancer. Her life could have been prolonged. Those who knew the woman put the blame on her for rejecting an objective and compassionate opinion from her physician. The doctor appeared to be gracious, even during her attacks on him.

My first response to any evaluation should be: Is it true? Is there anything constructive I may take from it? May I busy myself in such a way that I will not permit myself to be wounded? What may I do to make evaluation a regular and useful event in my professional experience?

LEADERS MAY EVALUATE
WHEN THEY ARE OBJECTIVE

Romanticists tend to find little or no fault in persons or programs. If they are "pollyanna" people they appear to be naive and incompetent among the burly sinners who run the world. They tend to make "good guys out of bad." They find no real evaluation of strengths and weaknesses for persons or situations.

Critics of Christians as leaders sometimes state that Christians are unwilling to set professional standards that must be subscribed to and kept—and if broken, some penalty or adjustment must be exacted. In the opinion of John Cheever, the eminent writer, there is a "lack of discrimination in Christian love." We are forced to acknowledge that many Christians do fail in discriminating human achievements so that they may be guilty of accepting inferior accomplishments. Analyses of artistic productions among Christians provide cases in point. Much of modern church music is ultra-simplistic, often banal, and transitory. However, it is doubtful that the popular Christian music is nearly as banal as the popular music scene of rock and roll or country music. Of course, there is excellence found in every musical idiom. We are here concerned with mass interests. Artistic culture in the general population is not high or memorable. We regret that popular musical idioms in the church are sometimes unsatisfactory when measured with that which is excellent. Better leadership by artists might improve cultural levels. Criticism of the right sort might also improve the culture.

Apparently many Christians never learn effective means for evaluation. Many do not feel it necessary. Others classify it with gossip and carping—carnal business. Christian leaders ought to learn effective

evaluation procedures and use them. Certainly the
Scriptures provide episodes of evaluation. A major duty of
the various prophets was to provide excellent criticism of
leaders and society. Even on personal and family matters
the prophets spoke. In the opening to 1 Kings the writer
accounts for Adonijah's attitudes through the omission of
nurture by his father, David. The evaluation was clear and
straightforward.

Nihilists tend to find little or no good in most of what
they observe. A basic weakness of radicals is the tendency
to tar everything as evil, except for the entirely new proposal the radicals would impose. Basic to radical policy is
to destroy, not reform, all that exists relative to their
concerns. They prefer that the system they oppose will
fall like an "overripe apple" into their hands. But events
seldom occur in such giveaway. No government can be
sufficiently improved for the radical. It must be
destroyed, likely through revolution or whatever violence,
so that the new ideal can be put in place.

It is a basic tenet of many socialist or communist
theorists that a democratic society is unfixable. It must be
destroyed even if a period of anarchy appears for a time so
that the decks are clear for the utopian scheme. Such
negation makes solutions nearly impossible. This
inflexibility of radicals usually dooms their cause. Citizens
are generally unwilling to tear down all they have built
**because part is defective. The best leaders know what
should be retained, repaired, rejected and introduced.**

An insightful analyst knows that good and ill are mixed.
Whatever we deal with contains both. Teachers know that
in a student's performance there is something to
commend and something else that needs improvement.
Both should be identified in order that the best may be
retained and strengthened, the weak may be improved or
eliminated. A literary critic knows there are, even in

classic works like those of Goethe or Shakespeare, both strong and weak features. Capitalism possesses benefits in its system, but it also has weaknesses. The church affirmatively contributes to quality in both social and church life, but it also fails in part. The analyst recognizes both the affirmatives and negatives in the case. If he is skillful he discovers the intensity and degree of the influence, and what may be done in light of the evidence.

Biblical narratives reveal strength and weakness in their characters, sometimes comparing persons, reciting situations that reveal them. It becomes a means of evaluation for self and service. Note the patterns in the narratives about Adam/Eve, Abraham/Sarah, Moses/Aaron, Jesus/disciples, Paul/Barnabas, Paul/John Mark, Paul/Timothy, or Paul/Peter, and many others.

Objective critics look for acceptable standards to measure the subject of their criticism. For example, one may utilize criteria based on some characteristics found in the nonleader. These include:

1. Defensiveness that grows out of personal insecurity.
2. Inflexibility that grows out of resistance to change.
3. Disorganization that grows out of unsureness about what ought to be done.
4. Hostility that grows out of rejection of human nature and conduct.

If a person is recommended for a position of leadership, and evaluation shows him to be somewhat defensive, inflexible, disorganized and hostile, that person is not going to be appointed. It is likely that an appointment to leadership would not only hurt the followers, but ultimately the appointee as well. His collapse as a leader, with the circumstances leading to the collapse, tend to embitter him.

LEADERS MAY EVALUATE
WHEN THEY PROFFER SOLUTIONS

It is the leader's duty to follow through to solutions. A critic should give pause to evaluation unless he seeks and suggests reasonable answers to problems he sees hovering over the institution. This policy applies to any institution from family to nation.

The evaluator either knows a reasonable direction to take or he can call upon someone who can be helpful. Here the problems pile up for both evaluators and those evaluated. What are the motives? Is genuineness present? Will there be follow-through? Are there sufficient resources? What are the time frames within which work can be done? What personnel will be at work? Is communication effective and complete? Other questions surface as events unfold. Problems are complex. Simplistic, off-the-cuff criticisms are not only insufficient, they are often harmful, contributing to lingering distress.

Solutions are themselves problems because people disagree, sometimes widely, on which solution or how much of it should be applied. There is commonly more disagreement about solutions than about problems they are supposed to meet. Problems are easier to find and describe; solutions are elusive. One of the most difficult assignments any follower has is to assist in applying a solution that is different from the one he would choose. Perhaps disillusionment was large motivation for Judas against Jesus. Judas preferred political and power solutions. Jesus preferred moral, spiritual and peaceful ones. Perhaps Peter began to implement the Judas expectation when, before the crucifixion, he lopped off a soldier's ear. Jesus healed the ear and taught again His peace. Facing the problem of differences between ourselves and our leaders, we may be assisted in remembering how many of the problems of Scripture were generated by similar tensions.

We try to resolve tension in various ways, sometimes by analyzing the motives of those in authority. If those motives are right, or we believe them to be, we tend to proceed, recognizing that responsibility rests heavily on others. Followers then ought to answer the questions: "Can this venture succeed if we do all we can to contribute to its implementation?" The answer may determine the extent of their involvement. That answer is vital for the leader, to put the plan in action.

Leaders, too, must ask themselves if their solutions are suitable to these followers. Human overload is a common problem. Following publication of Alvin Toffler's popular volume, *Future Shock*, the general population identifies with three areas of this overload: "sensory overstimulation," "cognitive overload," and "decisional stress." The three areas are well named, implying their own meanings, and express problems for leaders and followers before and since Toffler's statement.*

Sensory overstimulation is common. Currently the populace is barraged with material to hear, see, feel, smell and taste. We are "hyped up." The use of entertainment methods, even educational media, of colors, lights, speed, motion, and related stimulus sources is commonplace. The modern human being retreats from himself by losing some of his will and life perception in the psychedelic world whirring around him. Some of the retreat is involuntary.

Cognitive overload creates significant problems for individuals and society. Fire, war, murder, international exchange, oil and gas crises, election, rape, social change, family breakup, disease, hunger, abortion and

* Alvin Toffler, **Future Shock** (New York: Random House, 1970), p. 299ff.

what-have-you floods into our consciousness through various news sources. Many citizens simply cannot bear the weight of that kind and quantity of information. They flee to mountains, drop out, commit suicide, follow lives of no social worth, or the like. They may survive, but feel the world is collapsing all the time. Perhaps the collapse will affect them, or their loved ones. They feel they are living in perpetual tragedy. Things *seem* worse than ever. There is no peace. Stop the world: let me off.

Decisional stress is directly related to leadership. Problems are so large, stakes are so high, costs are so great, and conflict so prevalent, that decision making becomes a problem greater than many people will agree to take on. Expectations become too great. Fatigue takes the leader. He makes several poor decisions. He tries to live with them. He may lose his personal equilibrium. His family may break up. He may break.

It becomes my obligation to identify as part of the solution, in matters involving me. To do so well, I must be fairly well in control of myself, including my trend of mind and spirit. I must be willing to invest myself in some way in those areas of life important to me. At least they *should* be important to me. I should not sluff off.

Many people attack problems as children slap at puddles with sticks. The problems scatter and enlarge. This is common pattern in marriage problems. Some leave the problems to others, and do not vote or attend conferences where life- or community-influencing decisions are made. When things go wrong, the dropout spirits have no fair recourse. If they failed in their duty, they ought to accept what the activist has done.

When I was a young collegian, I found myself elected president of my class. In a later year, I was elected president of the student body in another college. In both offices I discovered that students had a fair idea about what leadership/followership was. Before anything could be done in either administration, I heard students remark, as they remarked in previous years, and many since, that student government would not accomplish anything, so why should students be interested? This is the most repeated criticism by students of their government. I analyzed the repeated observations.

Student governments may, and some do, accomplish a great deal. The problems of the faculty, trustees, and college administrations were not the problems of the students, except in those instances where issues overlapped. Many of the students stated their wish to take over this and that matter in college. But these were administration, or faculty, or trustee obligations. Few wished to define specific student concerns that could be analyzed and attacked. They chafed under the conflict of persons, ages, authorities, when they could have successfully dealt with problems whose boundaries were identified with students, rather than running interference against faculty, administration or trustee members. They could have improved their dormitories, newspapers, student aid programs, and the like. Business, personnel, curricula were duties of the university professionals. Students entered such areas by invitation. But what about **areas that were our own? They provided our proving ground if we would take them.**

One is impressed at leaders who focus on potential problems, and are creative to pose solutions before rather than after problems emerge. Perhaps no one else would solve the issues quite as they solve them. Such is creative leadership. Paul, the apostle, in a dramatic personal gesture, solved what might have become a problem. Knowing that those who pay the bills have a right to an accounting that would lead to evaluation, Paul foresaw potential problems for himself and the Corinthian church. He wished to carry through an enterprise involving his own burden and call. He did not wish to give an account or request permission for what he determined to do. He might introduce controversy at a time when the church ought to be treating other matters. So he took himself off the Corinthian church payroll. Although he had the right to accept the support of the church, and he defended that right so as to protect it for others, he would not accept it for himself. He made his own living so that he could maintain a broad ministry with Jews and Gentiles, with persons in all stations and places. The Corinthians might restrict his activities.

Characteristics

As suggested several times in this chapter, evaluation is most objective when it is based on predetermined standards. In that way there are few surprises, there is less likelihood that one will feel he is being mistreated, misjudged, or treated with prejudice.

When criticism is done on high, even scholarly, levels, there is commonly an authoritative and agreed-upon standard by which the evaluation is to be made. In rhetorical criticism an evaluator chooses to review the work of an eminent speaker. The evaluator may be quite inferior in his own abilities as a speaker, but he can readily evaluate this orator if he is thorough and perceptive in the treatment of his subject. If the speaker is to be evaluated on the criteria of the classical principles of Aristotle, principles extant in *De Rhetorica*, the critic must well know that rhetoric and well know the speeches as well as the circumstances related to the orator and his speaking. The evaluator does not merely give his opinion, but what has occurred in a speaking situation in the light of a body of excellent published principles. Those expectations are available to the speaker, if he is diligent to find them.

Some of the characteristics we should look for in the leader/manager, characteristics which, if fulfilled, make for effectiveness, are:

1. *A feeling of responsibility.* A leader should feel the weight of whatever is to be done. That weight cannot be too heavy or he will collapse, or in some way evade the duty. But the weight must not be too light for him, or he will take the responsibility too casually, skipping steps and using insufficient resources and personnel to accomplish purposes. Easy assignments, neglected, fail as certainly as difficult ones do. Duties must be properly weighed if success is to crown efforts.

2. *A determination of moral courage.* A leader should feel strongly about the rightness of his course. He may not be physically robust, but courage is a strength of character. By believing in what he is doing sufficiently to put himself "on the line," to take appropriate risks, the leader provides credibility for what he is doing and thereby inspires others who admire courage, even though they may not have it in themselves.

3. *A will to go through.* A leader should believe that if the project is worth launching it is worth completing. To complete it he must take all the steps to conclusion. One of the leading evidences that a person is not a leader is that he is unwilling in a worthy cause to go all the way to the end. He "tires of the greatness of his way." He may be an effective "start-up" man but retreats at some point crucial to success. He is not a leader, although a leader can well use his skills. (If, after launching, a project is seen by thoughtful critics as misbegotten or untimely or in some way ill-advised, it ought to be dropped. But this is not the fault of leadership. In fact, leadership recognizes the wisdom of aborting a cause when circumstances suggest it.)

4. *A measure of good judgment.* A leader should know boundaries. He knows the differences between credible and incredible, between plausible and implausible. There is reason to believe his venture can succeed. Odds vary

and change along the way so that a plausible project becomes implausible, or vice versa. The leader can adjust accordingly to begin, abort, or change course.

5. *An alertness in thought.* A leader should know how to think clearly. He perceives immediate and long range action and meaning. He knows directions. He feels he knows the conclusion toward which these actions tend. And he is alert to deviation. What will get the purpose off the track?

6. *A thoroughness in action.* A leader should maintain effort in every department. He knows how to track. He remembers that "for the want of a nail...the war was lost." Incredible as the story is, the Diablo Canyon atomic energy generator plant in California, costing more than a billion dollars, was prevented from opening because engineers unwittingly reversed installation of safety equipment. Someone failed, and the error stood until a young engineer in his mid-twenties pointed it out on the eve of opening full tests. Students of leadership are rightly appalled at the failures of management in such instances.

7. *A zeal for his institution.* A leader must be optimistic about his cause, his people, and the institution he represents. Realistic about its strengths and weaknesses, he believes that this institution deserves his best efforts and those of others.

8. *An enterprise to improve.* A leader knows human effort can be improved, often greatly improved. If something works well we rightly are reluctant to change it. An excellent mechanic once warned me, "If it works, don't fix it." But some things are not working well, or not as well as they should. Through evaluation these problem areas may be found. The best leaders and followers wish to improve. It was an exasperated Winston Churchill who said, "If you simply take up the attitude of defending it there will be no hope of improvement."

Without evaluation in our lives, we will not likely do

what we ought to do, either in quality or quantity of effort. But some persons feel they cannot bear the scrutiny and evaluation of another. They interpret it as gossip or as emotional blows they are unable to absorb. When I was a young faculty member, the college in which I was teaching tried to develop professional approaches to the life and practices of the institution. One procedure proposed to the faculty was to initiate student evaluations of each teacher. By means of a simple questionnaire circulated to the students in various classes, faculty members could discover the perceptions of their classes by students. One woman refused the proposal for her classes. She admitted openly that she "couldn't take it" to have students make negative comments about her work.

My teacher-colleague would have become a better teacher than she was had she been willing to subject herself to the exercise. She was an excellent teacher, but was low in esteem for her own performance. Student responses would have been far more positive and commendatory than she realized. The areas needing improvement would be fewer than she feared. Almost always affirmations for us are larger than negations. It is simply that we find one fault to be more of an attention-getter in us than many virtues.

If we can accept evaluation in our lives for what it is, we are bound to improve. If no evaluation is given, our improvement will be fitful and spasmodic, if it occurs at all. Workers who feel cheated in not receiving evaluations of their performance have good reason to feel so. They tend to believe their supervisors do not care about them or their work except as the company or institution is profited directly.

The conclusion of the matter is judgment about the quality of leadership available to us. When that has been determined, we decide to follow, or not to follow, or to follow in part, this leader. We determine the characteristics that are important to us to make our judgments.

Without evaluation of performance, neither leaders nor followers can be sure they are doing as they ought. It is easy to slip off track so even interim evaluations must also be made. Thoroughness, objectivity, and compassion must be incorporated. Even then there are those who feel they cannot receive evaluation. Threat looms too large for them. They should give up hope to lead a democratic body. But if the leader, and those who lead with him as well as those who follow, will accept evaluation of themselves and their performances, all that relates to what they do will likely improve. At the least, efficiency improves. At the last, most participants will be pleased.

—5—

The Priorities of Leadership

PEOPLE

...furthering the administration of God...the goal of our instruction is love from a pure heart and a good conscience and a sincere faith....I write so that you may know how one ought to conduct himself in the household of God....In pointing out these things to the brethren, you will be a good servant of Christ Jesus....For God has not given us a spirit of timidity, but of power and love and discipline....

—1 and 2 Timothy, NASB

Leaders do both well and poorly, just as engineers, or artists, or truckdrivers, or teachers do in their performances. Leadership, even the most commendable, does not guarantee success. More factors than leadership and followership influence life and institutional situations. Perhaps leadership in a losing cause may be more creative and admired than in a winning cause. Robert E. Lee seems to have been a better leader in the American Civil War, given the limits of his **resources, than William McClellan or even Ulysses S. Grant. Grant benefited from a larger base and greater** firepower. And he had a more cohesive government behind him. Abraham Lincoln yearned for a northern general to match Lee. Grant was the closest he came to Lee.

A leader, especially in a democratic society, owes it to prospective followers to make known his purposes and values. In the assumption that projected purposes and designated values are clear and acceptable to an adequate number of followers, the best leader will show himself competent in five skills: planning, organizing, coordinating, leading and evaluating. These are joined together by communication grids sufficient for project purposes.

Leadership is difficult to assess. For like much else related to human behavior, leadership factors are not discreet from each other, and they relate to other factors in situations. Leadership is a compound, not an independent element. There are many variables, and what suits one situation does not serve another. While analyzing a factor, the insightful critic is aware he may be sublimating another factor, or appear to be violating it. We often, in discussion, choose to isolate a factor, make general observations about it, knowing we are not saying all that needs be said. We know, too, that in some circumstances our analysis will prove inadequate or even untrue. Therefore, discussion of leadership becomes difficult. What is workable here is unworkable there. Such is the matter of human dynamics. Therefore we suggest rather than pontificate; we risk rather than take "sure things."

Human differences alone create problems for would-be leaders. These are well illustrated in the reviews given by Dennis Guernsey and others to the response of individuals in marriages and families to leadership. Guernsey quotes four personality categories: 1) movers, 2) followers, 3) resisters, 4) bystanders. He treats each one perceptively. Movers start things, give orders, provide directions. Followers tend to accept orders and suggestions, going along with movers. Resisters, for their own reasons, respond negatively to nearly everything, digging in their heels. Bystanders watch the passing scene, creating distance between themselves and those who are participating.

No person fits totally in one category. At times he fulfills the definition of each, but one dominates him. Distribution of the factors in us is reality for everyone, creating complications for families and society. We know that movers/followers/resisters/bystanders intermarry and have children. Their own personal plot, for many persons, becomes too complicated for them to sift through. They may wonder about who they are, and what they have gotten into. Faultfinding is common in these situations.

Different problems are likely to arise from the above combinations. Guernsey's concern was to find out what happens when movers marry movers, or marry followers, or marry resisters, or marry bystanders. What happens when followers marry followers, or marry resisters, or marry bystanders? What happens when resisters marry resisters, or marry bystanders? Finally, what happens when bystanders marry bystanders? The answers are intriguing and enlightening. They may provide microcosms of what happens in larger social enterprises.

One of the most enlightening is Guernsey's challenge of the common belief that the biblical meaning of leadership, as traditionally interpreted, in the family is the husband as mover, and the wife as follower. Granting that marriages in this combination are generally happy, solid ones, Guernsey rejects the tendency of Christians so married to assume that all others should be designed exactly in the same mold. Because a man may have been made a follower in the dynamics of his paternal family, he will not automatically become a mover upon marriage. A woman made a mover, perhaps because her parents were both followers, thereby forcing her in childhood and youth to become a mover, will not automatically become a follower when she marries.

Leadership in a family is not stereotyped by a simple formula of a mover (male) and a follower (female). We do better to see Jesus as following the leadership of His human parents, so that He gains an integrity for leadership of the special group of disciples and any others who would follow Him. And we may learn that a marriage constructed on husband/father leadership, wife/mother submission, and child obedience—all founded on love—is typical of God's pattern of work and social control, but that does not mean other marriage patterns fail, or that they violate the biblical ideal. That ideal does not mean that other patterns are either wrong or unworkable.

PERSONAL LEADERSHIP

Everyone has a philosophy of life. That philosophy may be simplistic and undeveloped. If my stepfather had been asked about his philosophy of life, he would have been embarrassed. He did not know the meaning of the word "philosophy." But I could construct his philosophy, having watched him for many years and hearing his words. He lived by it with intense consistency. Anyone knowing my stepfather would fairly well know how to conduct himself in his presence.

The philosophy of life constructed for themselves by Will and Ariel Durant was carefully wrought. They fairly well lived it out, except for their views favoring socialism in government. It found extended statement in several of their writings, as in *The Lessons of History* and *A Dual Biography*. They wended their ways through religion, science, politics, travel, literature, history, and experience to state their position. Sophisticated, sometimes urbane, sometimes reclusive, sometimes involved, sometimes escapist, the Durants put their case, their philosophy of life by which they interpreted the great story of philosophy in civilization.

It is not likely that the Durant personal philosophy was more effective than that of my illiterate stepfather. Will Durant would say as much in writing about his father, Joseph:

I have known some gracious gentlemen, but I have never known a better man. Thinking of him, I wonder whether an illiterate person of good character, who becomes a good husband and a good father, is of more worth to a community than a man of much education, assiduous reasoning, and ten thousand books.*

A philosophy provides, in the everyday sense of the term, a guideline for living. It may not deal with the great issues of the philosophers, persons who wrestle with the nature of man and the universe, the problems of epistemology or the ideal state. But even a simple man has some idea about the boundaries of his life, and the extent of his beliefs. For anyone, including himself, to go beyond those boundaries creates alarm for him. He wishes to get back, and to have those he cares about with him. In this way he feels, or hopes, his philosophy is sufficiently comprehensive, able to treat everything entering his life. It gives him a feeling of balance. When a philosophy (view of life) is comprehensive, or believed to be, it is expected to meet all normal situations, even crises, to maintain life balance.

When a philosophy becomes one's own, it seems to be as much a part of the person as his viscera. He carries that mental life perception with him all the time. It cannot be removed like clothing. It seems to permeate all that he is and does, as well as that he wants to be, even if he never achieves his vision. Out of his personal philosophy, commitments may be made and kept. At least he hopes he can keep them. A sense of worth grows up in him, becoming stronger if his life view becomes large and firm, roomy enough to account for his experiences. It is even better for him when it accounts also for the experiences of others, especially for those around him in his family and professional life.

Like personal goals, a personal philosophy is firmer,

---

* Will and Ariel Durant, **A Dual Autobiography** (New York: Simon and Schuster, 1977), p. 28.

more useful and effective for a person if he writes it out in full. It is amended from time to time, improving in composition as it focuses more on life meaning. Organization improves the statement, but more, it improves performance. It is best when everything in life has meaning to the author of the statement.

RESPONDING

In the call to act or respond, one feels like "yes" or "no" or "maybe." To avoid direct decision making, we may do just about anything, even pretending we did not hear any question or do not know that one is before us to be resolved. Perhaps half the issues that come before us will resolve themselves. They only require time and space. With that much success (50 percent) and so little effort (delay only), we may find it easy to fall into a habit of procrastination.

Procrastination is not leadership. Many issues, and the most important ones, seldom go away. Leadership means resolution, resolution in time frames to gain the best results possible, given the circumstances of the matter.

I found it difficult for many years to make a negative decision involving my personal involvement in some endeavor. I could agree to do something very quickly if I felt the answer should be affirmative. But I made various devious responses to other requests when, in truth, I believed the responses should have been turn-downs. The most common reply was delay: "See me a week from today," or "Maybe, but I will talk it over with my wife." So the delaying tactic would ease the burden both for myself and the person asking for action. There were other easy ways out. Where appropriate to do so, my most common tactic was to make a small financial contribution to the cause. It is an easy way to avoid personal involvement and time investment. But none of this was leadership on my part.

Not until I learned the essential guidelines of my personal decision-making processes did I find or save time for myself and for those who looked to me for participation, especially the participation of leadership. It continues to distress me to say "no." But it is a necessary response for persons who cannot take on additional responsibility. They prove, in such cases, they know something about leadership.

Many men and women have composed lists of criteria on which they cast both themselves and the decision they must make. Writing in *The Toastmaster*, E.J. Radican listed questions that persons may use to determine their response to requests to do volunteer work:

1. Do I really want to do it?
2. What will I gain personally?
3. Will my family benefit?
4. Will I have a chance to do this again?
5. Can it be done quickly?
6. How much help will I get?
7. Am I being asked because I always say yes?
8. Will I have to neglect family and friends to do this thing?
9. What commitments and activities must I cancel to do this?

Some of the questions may appear to be selfish, such as, "What will I gain personally?" If the gain would be financial, I may not do it because it might well hold ethical considerations. Or the financial benefit may be appropriate as partial fulfillment in an otherwise voluntary situation. If I could learn something new, I might be willing to do as requested, when I would otherwise refuse the request.

A family might benefit by all members participating, or, to the contrary, the family might have to pay dearly for the participating of either mother or father. So the request is decided on personal grounds.

If the project must be extended, interference with other projects might make this one out of the question. If it can be completed in a short period, it may be feasible.

Evaluating guidelines, and receiving favorable answers to them, I ought to affirm my willingness to take on an opportunity with enthusiasm, providing leadership to the best of my ability to carry through the assignment. I would make it a duty to enjoy, with the purpose to succeed.

TIME MANAGEMENT

Time is an inevitable limiting factor in anything we do, in all of life. Resources (amount available) and personnel (varying effectiveness) are sometimes limiting factors in business or commerce, but time is *always* limiting. How do we perceive time and manage it, in ourselves and for the purpose of leadership?

Philosophy of Time

How much time should be given to this or that? To answer, by way of analogy—the only thing one may do to manage a hundred dollar bill is to break it up into change: ones, fives, tens, twenties, perhaps a fifty, and silver. The hundred is all there is of it. How should the parts totaling $100 be spent? Therein is the secret. And it applies to time. I have no more than each day of my life. How will I divide it, and for what purpose will I invest each part? At the least, consideration of time and its effective management is a life-saving matter. No leader in worthy causes can expect to accomplish his purposes without effective control of both his time and the time of others, his followers.

This concern leads to diagnosis. How do I use my time? To begin, I assume something is amiss in the way I utilize my conscious hours. If one maintains a daily log, in a calendar divided into 15-minute periods, he will soon discover how well or poorly his time is invested. The time taken to keep the log is more than returned in the time saved after learning where to conserve and reorder it. Perhaps no other proposal for practical action is more widely agreed upon by writers on the subject than this one about discovering what is nonproductive in time consumption.

Do activities in my life deserve the time investment they receive? Various means are recommended for evaluating time-eaters. At the close of each day I may evaluate each quarter hour, awarding each with a 1, 2, or 3. If "1," the time was invested in the right thing for that period. If "2," the event was worthwhile, even necessary, but could have been treated more effectively at some other time. If "3," the thing itself was useless, perhaps it was wrong. At least it was inappropriate for me to do it. Someone else might do it better and with greater satisfaction.*

Managing Time

An important matter is to find wasted time in the past and prevent waste in the future. Time is wasted from lack of system or foresight. For example, a person discovers that he has a habit of losing time through repetitive crisis occurrences. He seldom, if ever, has time to plan, to guide matters rather than be forced by them. If one is seldom on top of his life and problems, he must assume that he is either overextended or he is not using his time well.

---

* **Effective Time Management**, (Englewood Cliffs, New Jersey: Prentice Hall, Inc.)

In organizations the problems multiply to steal time. Time is sometimes wasted from overstaffing. Overstaffing is more common than understaffing in many businesses. The loss of awareness of how much a person can and ought to do is cause for considerable disappointment in men and women with their jobs. In the recessional period beginning in 1980, both Canada and the United States discovered how inefficient both government and business had become through overstaffing.

Time is wasted from poor organization. Evidence appears in excessive numbers of meetings by managers. Simple policies might well treat problems, and treat them with equity that is often lost in meeting. Efficient organizations develop effective policies, and those who work for them follow those policies, or make approaches to get them changed. Policies are often either unknown by affected employees, or are disregarded in some way.

Time is wasted from malfunction in information systems. Evidence appears in the lack of distribution of needed information or wrong information. In some instances information does not get through because it is poorly communicated in media. Sloppy materials sent out or casual treatment given by persons who are supposed to be leading their people spell *inefficiency*. Such leaders seem not to lead.

Consolidating Time

An important matter for anyone is to find discretionary time. What is available for use? First duty is to set schedules for specific duties. What must be done? That which is required should be scheduled without any question. Priorities must be set and periodically reviewed. If they are not, the leader as well as his followers will be caught up in the "tyranny of the immediate." They become controlled rather than controlling. They can become occupied with rattles in the vehicle rather than the functioning of the machinery.

Christian leaders, even some secular ones, often reserve an early daily period at home for themselves. In that period they not only build up their quality of life in devotional exercises, principally reading and prayer, but they learn how to meditate, to commune with themselves about their own development, their day, their concerns. They know that, given time and adequate treatment, most problems are soluble. Jesus implied as much when He said, "Are there not twelve hours in the day?" The question inspires belief that there is time to do whatever we ought to do.

The creative person never feels he has enough time. One feature of his creativity is to work at finding discretionary time. He can do that through ongoing analysis. As already suggested, he may keep a log of his activities. Not only does he plan in advance, but he evaluates what he does after he does it. The exercise does not take much time, nor does it require significant insight. The fact that he will never have enough time to do all his imagination urges him to do, that he will yield to undue pressures when he does not have firm control of his own destiny, that he will leave out of his life those activities and involvements important to him and his family—all these should drive him to personal time management.

Surprisingly, leaders are often skillful at professional time management and poor at personal time control. Family and friends are astonished that they have such high discipline for professional life and so little for personal. In such instances there are other factors to consider.

The take-charge leader, like Frank Bunker Gilbreth, whose way of life was described in *Cheaper By The Dozen*, carries his ideas over into all of his experience. The efficiency that he taught to others he followed with zeal in everything he did. The family enjoyed the way their husband/father carried his ideas through. On his death his wife picked up his leadership for herself. She believed she had a fine teacher.

The leader who bifurcates his life into personal and professional, using professional life to carry through his ideals on leadership and his personal life to escape the pressure and constant attention to duty, may not appear to his family to be a leader at all. He leaves all matters to his wife for social events, for management of family affairs. He is comfortable in following, having filled up psychic vessels on his job. This may or may not be a good thing for the family. If the wife is a leader, there is base for the husband to gain his respite from duties of leadership. The wife fulfills herself, depending upon the balances between her approach, her husband's, and that of the children and friends. Two "movers" have married. All may be well. As intimated earlier, this does not mean that the father is not the "head of his home." Perhaps we miss the concept of leadership in that domestic sense when we assume the leader is a take-charge person, that he has felicity for saying "no" and making it stick, that he has an element of the autocrat in him. But the leader of the family, in the biblical sense, is basically a model, a model in the tradition of Jesus, inspiring his family through strength, knowledge and character. From these virtues he leads. Without virtues, he leads his family poorly.

THE UNLEADER

As one approaches the closing years of his professional life, he reminisces about the success or lack of success in himself and his lifetime acquaintances, especially college classmates. A review of old college yearbooks inspires inevitable questions. What happened to him? to her? When we were students we believed that these would become leaders, and these would not. We were partly right, we were partly wrong. Many of the prospective leaders did not make the grade, and some we believed would not achieve as leaders did so. What factors made any difference?

One of the major factors for leadership failure is procrastination—the pseudo-art of "putting things off." Those who made the grade as leaders were sufficiently industrious that they did their detail work. At first they did it themselves. Later, they may have delegated most of it, but even then they made sure it was done. They were not listless or languid in carrying out their duties and taking responsibility. They did not assume too much that others would do all they were assigned to do.

Certainly, it is easy to procrastinate. Dante described the matter well: "Hesitating I remain at war 'twixt will and will not in my thought." In the natural we are lazy people, even indolent and slothful. The sure sign of an unleader is his chronic way of postponing and not doing an unpleasant task, or one that seems unimportant to him, but is important in the scheme of things. It may be one somebody else was supposed to have done and failed to do. If the purpose is to succeed, the leader must make up the omission in some way.

Procrastinators advance numerous excuses to justify their weakness. They wait for a better time, for an inspiration, for more information, or the like. For most procrastinators the time, the inspiration, the additional help do not materialize. Their excuses for failure are never good enough. For example, the chronically late person complains that he is late because he has no sense of time. This is patently untrue. If he had no sense of time, he would as often be too early as he is too late—his lateness would not be so consistent. The latecomer has a sort of plan at work. If he did not, why is he always about 15 or 20 minutes late?

Procrastinators do not rightly steer their lives—they seem to drift. They find themselves at some port sufficiently often that they may survive in a world where there are other drifting workers. So survival is taken as life's norm. At best it is a languid life, if not fully pleasing or happy. The experience of living fully, abundantly, is not known. That they might be leaders, achievers, is not seriously considered, therefore not taken as a lively option. They long ago "gave up."

THE CHRISTIAN LEADER

In the text introducing this chapter, a selection of phrases from 1 and 2 Timothy, the apostle Paul sought to teach his protégé, Timothy, about administration. The apostle was first concerned with the genuineness of the leader as an ethical person, and his purpose to teach purity of heart, excellence of conscience, and sincerity of faith—all in a context of love. From this ideal one learns proper Christian conduct. In the context there are specifics to be pointed out for the purpose of making a "good servant [follower of a leader] of Jesus Christ." A leader who sets out to accomplish this purpose is not "timid" but is a person of "power," "love," and "discipline." These characteristics are requirements for the complete Christian leader. They are made practical in the development of one's philosophy; an ability to make decisions based on knowledge of God and self, as well as the facts of problem situations; and a willingness to manage time in effective ways.

Many recent books and articles on leadership, management and success accent the importance of values, shared values, in persons and institutions. Authors point out how companies and families thrive when leaders and followers hold to and implement an idealism. Some writers call these values religious. They tie the values to the leaders, and the leaders to the values.

—6—

The Promise of Leadership SUCCESS

Then I said unto them, Ye see the distress that we are in, how Jerusalem lieth waste, and the gates thereof are burned with fire: come let us build up the wall of Jerusalem, that we be no more a reproach.

—Nehemiah 2:17

Most persons hold at least mild belief that they possess leadership potential if only they were called upon to exercise it. Nearly all do hold some leadership qualities, awaiting only an appropriate, even if modest, situation to utilize them. Most persons can lead, if they will, in ordinary life situations like those created in the family. Even so, many fail.

When leadership becomes a topic of discussion we generally think about larger matters than family life. The majority of men and women feel they cannot take on large social duties. In their estimation, circumstances as well as their natures would not permit. Nevertheless, in those special situations for which they are suited, they should expect to try and succeed at the purpose of leadership.

We wrongly assume that intelligence identifies successful leaders. Peter Drucker in his studies found no correlation between a person's effectiveness and his intelligence.* Numerous illustrations might be cited to demonstrate leadership failure among creative people. Thomas Edison engineered many inventions, but marketed poorly. Henry Ford manufactured automobiles and sold them, but was slow to incorporate improvements and was overtaken in sales by General Motors. His leadership failed at several important junctures.

Acknowledged leaders, perhaps with eminent historical

* Peter F. Drucker, **The Effective Executive** (New York: Harper and Row Publishers, 1967), p. 1.

rank, might totally fail in important areas. Was it not Winston Churchill who fancied himself a great financier? During one work week he presumed to prove his prowess as a bear on Wall Street. Using Bernard Baruch's office, he purchased and sold stocks, only to lose what money he had by week's end. Fortunately for him, Baruch secretly bought whatever Churchill sold, and sold whatever he purchased so that at the end of the debacle Churchill had his money back and was somewhat humbled at his inability to lead the financial world.

Bernard Baruch, masterful market manager and taken as a leading advisor to several American presidents, was sometimes chided that he never stood for election to public office. He never risked himself at the polls. Perhaps Baruch knew more about himself than his contemporaries knew about him—that his special qualities of leadership could never succeed in a political arena.

Astute analysts who have closely observed clergymen try to find why some succeed and others fail. Ministers are supposed to be leaders. Those who fail in leadership are not necessarily bad men. They seldom are. They may be more righteous than others who succeed in comparable situations. They may not know what to do, may not have the energy to do what must be done, may not have the heart or personality for the venture. They may not possess large vision. Their timing may be off. They may not know how to relate to people in cooperative situations. As suggested earlier in a common truism, many factors relate to success and failure in leader situations, religious or secular. To be true to self and faithful to the cause is not nearly enough, even if important beginning considerations.

When each of us looks into a mirror, what is seen? A writer suggests that we cast our impressions in animal terms to understand our personalities and what we may do. We might gain better perceptions of why we act in ways we do, or not act at all, or why people react to us as they do. We stereotype the animals to accomplish our purpose. For example, investors on Wall Street in New York are often classified as "bulls" and "bears." A popular advertisement for a brokerage house stated that it was "bullish on America." It was dynamic and active in the market.

Do I see in myself a rooster, or pig, or butterfly, or bull, or stallion, or some other representative creature? Do I see differences in that perception from day to day? Do my colleagues receive different impressions? So a view of myself becomes dramatic, and might well assist me in planning a successful leadership role. What am I like? What promise do I give?

LEADERSHIP GENERATES SUCCESS THROUGH STYLE

What is the style of leadership I will follow? In what environment, real or imagined, will I cast it? What do I believe, or what is my faith, that makes a difference? What is my largest assumption? What other assumptions do I hold?

Each leader labors within large assumptions. The ethics of Confucius were constructed on a presupposition about the integrity of the family. No wonder then that the family was held in so high regard in the orient for many centuries. It was basic to belief in social and personal order. Only recently has it weakened. The philosophy of Pascal was built upon total confidence in God. The philosophy of John Dewey was built upon a belief that man was entirely dependent upon himself in personal and social contexts. To accept any of these viewpoints a person is bound to a set of presuppositions traced back from his positions on issues.

In democratic societies, and in a time when extensive knowledge has become important to effective leadership, assumptions are emerging that were formerly overlooked. Those assumptions are revealing themselves in changes of attitudes, educational principles, politics, opinions about man and his involvement in life activity. For example, the modern leader must assume that he will involve his people in the leadership process. He is not a person who alone decides and requires followers to acquiesce.

Our concern in this section is with historical and democratic change that indicates new types of leadership. It is the development of acceptable styles of leadership from rugged and admired individuals of the past to the current broader approach of teams and coaches who lead among equals in problem solving. What is our hope, and what is the promise of its fulfillment?

Fortune Magazine, in 1976, published a profile of the 500 chief executives of principal businesses. The new profile represented a break with traditional concepts, and indicates the development of a new style of leader. The following table contrasts the executive of one generation to that of another.*

FIGURE SIX

Executive profile

(*Fortune* magazine)

	1976	1950
1. Background	From middle class	From wealthy class
2. Training	Formal business college degrees, 50%	About 30% took some college
3. Age	Younger average age	

---

* Charles G. Burck, "A Group Profile of the Fortune 500 Chief Executives," **Fortune**, Vol. 93, May 1976, p. 173ff.

FIGURE SIX: Executive profile [cont'd]

	1976	1950
4. Politics	Unpredictable— many are independents	Three-fourths Republicans
5. Religion	Unpredictable—1/5 are Episcopalian. Catholics, Jews and Lutherans increasing. Jews high and Catholics low.	WASP high with Episcopalians 1/3 of force
6. Sex	Male dominance. Some women.	Male
7. Race	White	White
8. Social	Unpredictable	Superior - Patrician
9. Theory	Middle-roader	Conservative
10. Difficulty levels	Harder to do job	Easier to do job
11. Government	Increased control	Less control
12. Esteem (public)	Lower	Higher

Effectiveness

Leaders are, in our time, sometimes cast as managers, executives, chairpersons, or the like. Remember, advised Peter Drucker, an executive is not concentrating so much on "doing things right," as "getting the right things done." "Intelligence, imagination, and knowledge" are essential resources, but only effectiveness converts them into results. The leader may not be *highly* intelligent, but he knows how to draw upon the intellectual resources of others. It is largely agreed that "super intelligence" is not necessary in the leader. But he must be a person of good judgment.

In modern times effective executives are especially needed because of "knowledge workers." Formerly most persons were "manual workers." Production was easy to measure, decisions were relatively simple. So emphasis was placed on doing things right instead of getting the right things done. The issue was efficiency in producing units of the product. Currently leadership requires effectiveness in "knowledge work," or mind meeting mind rather than mind (leader) meeting hand (manual worker). In the new approach even the manual worker has useful mental input for his job.

Until recently the domination of operations and production manuals was clearly seen. Persons were told what to do. Matters were rather clearly staked out. Drucker reminds us: "Lincoln's Secretary of War had fewer than fifty civilian subordinates, most of them...telegraph clerks."* Around 1903 the entire U.S. government under Theodore Roosevelt in Washington, D.C., could be housed in one building on the mall today. Hospitals had no technicians, but were run by a few doctors and nurses who did all professional work relating to knowledge. Today the center of gravity is on the knowledge worker. So effectiveness is the issue. Yardsticks for manual work cannot be used for knowledge work. Knowledge workers, for example, cannot be so closely supervised. They must be evaluated on their achievements. How they get there may differ from one to the other.

New knowledge, ideas, information are the products of knowledge workers. These then must be converted somewhere into necessary or helpful behavior and action to have meaning. Drucker stated:

---

* Drucker, pp. 1-9.

Education is the one area...in which the richest of all
societies, the United States, has a genuine
advantage—provided it can make the knowledge
worker productive. And productivity for the
knowledge worker means the ability to get the right
things done. It means effectiveness.*

Executives (leaders) have responsibility for, and
authority over, the direction, content and quality of work
to be done or methods of performance in their businesses.
This knowledge work is not usually defined by quantity or
cost, but by results. One man may succeed with results,
whereas in another company two hundred men fail.

An executive may be anyone who by virtue of position or
knowledge makes decisions in the normal course of his
work that have significant impact on the performance and
results of the group. He must plan, organize, integrate,
motivate and measure. We remind ourselves again that
there is authority of knowledge as there is authority of
position. Authority of position is no longer exclusive.

Knowledge workers functioning outside an organization may have less concern for leadership/followership
than those within. A physician is effective by focusing on
a patient's needs. He has only limited corporate matters
to consider. To aid healing and comfort the patient is his
priority order. But the executive in an organization is
pushed toward nonresults by: 1) the intrusions upon his
time, intrusions over which he has little control; 2) the
tendency on his part to "operate" the whole organization
rather than deal with specific purposes; 3) the
acquiescence to events, permitting them to run him rather
than following set criteria for his work; 4) the dominance
of the organization in which other idea workers are out of
phase with him so that his work may not be used; and 5)
the captivity within the organization which distorts or

---

* Ibid., p. 5.

blocks information from the outside world so that efforts
and costs are not turned into revenues and benefits.

Some of these factors, undetected by a company, have
led to significant errors. For example, during the late 1950s
the Ford Motor Company launched a new model car, the
Edsel, which was rejected by the public. It was a monumental failure. The organization distorted and blocked
information that might well have made a difference.

Our concern should not only be with trends but changes
in trends. The mechanical moron known as a computer is
a logic machine, but man, who is often illogical, is
perceptive. Had the computer-spawned Edsel been
subject to the perceptions of knowledgeable and wise men
at Ford, manufacture may never have begun, or under
way, may have been given a turn for success. The factual
material fed into the "Edsel program" would have been
moderated by the concerns of experienced men who could
not translate what they knew into computer language.

Executives in the late twentieth century are often
contemptuous of information or stimulus that cannot be
reduced to computer language. These persons are
insulated from the outside world with its perceptions.
With all the good that computers return to man, they
cannot lead. They lack sudden flexibility, and they
cannot, with all their speed, keep up in decision making.
Between the input and the read-out and the decision,
changes have taken place. Life is that fast in a
technological age.

Effectiveness can be learned. If society were dependent
upon gifted executives, only those possessing natural
endowments, that society would be doomed. There are
too many executives needed to rely on gifted persons
alone. There is no one effective "personality" for an
executive anyway.* The common factor Drucker found in

---

* Note Drucker's description, p. 22.

variant executives was in *practices* that make those leaders effective. He wrote: "Effectiveness...is a habit; that is, a complex of practices. And practices can always be learned." They have to be mastered by repetition *ad nauseam*. Even great pianists would not do well if they did not practice their scales, which is what beginners do.

These leadership practices relate to: 1) using time, 2) getting results, 3) building on strengths, 4) concentrating on major areas, and 5) making effective decisions. But the list may be lengthened to cover a greater number of characteristics for different types of leadership. Such a list also requires interpretation. Whether he knows it or not, a leader holds an assumption or predisposition to a certain approach to leadership: autocratic, democratic, delegated, status given or whatever. Each has special characteristics. Each might succeed: each might fail.

Leadership Styles

Students of leadership sometimes make erroneous sweeping value judgments regarding leadership styles. Some potential followers dislike democratic leadership. They respond efficiently and with appreciation to firm and autocratic types. Their rearing, their experiences, perhaps their very chemistry have much to do with a leadership style they like and respond to. Even national styles are sometimes used as criteria for seeking leadership. This perception explains much of what has happened in history, is happening and will happen again. Hitler was welcomed by many German citizens and hated by others. It is likely that autocratic leaders like Hitler, Stalin, Mussolini were the types their people in majority wanted at the time. This preference does not mean that misuse of power by leaders, or their personal failure and prejudices were condoned by their followers. Autocratic leadership can be ethical, humane and effective. The issue is: do we wish to have that kind of leadership even when it can be shown to be effective? A democracy replies, "No!"

In Christian contexts there is sharp disagreement about what leadership is and which type of leadership is "God-ordained." Biblical narratives suggest different types of leadership without implying superiority in one or the other. Apparently a form or pattern of leadership is acceptable if it serves humane purposes and is useful to followers. Followers of one pattern of ecclesiastical leadership may find another totally unsatisfactory, and the followers of the second reject the first. It is common, in moving from church to church, for an itinerant minister to find in one a congregation-led church, and a pastor-dominated one in another, with both succeeding.

Perhaps comparisons between two types of leadership will assist. They follow below. Statements are not exclusive. We might do better with more discreet models suggesting mixes in concepts. Categories are not mutually exclusive as they seem to be here in bold statements. But we can readily sense the illusion of different kinds of leadership in the comparisons.

FIGURE SEVEN

Autocratic leader vs. person leader

	Autocratic Leader	*Person Leader*
1. Authority	Maintains lines of authority. Uses chain of command. He rules, perhaps with "divine authority."	Chief among equals. Uses systems such as teacher and disciples.

FIGURE SEVEN: Autocratic leader vs. person leader [cont'd]

	Autocratic Leader	Person Leader
2. Knowledge	Leader knows best and informs followers, perhaps with commands. He casts himself as a teacher and ahead of others.	Leader focuses large picture but leaves obligations to others for the partials. He casts himself as a learner.
3. Focus	Everyone works for the leader. (Presumably his purpose deserves the dedication of all.)	Greatest leader is the servant among followers. (The welfare of followers is a vital matter.)
4. Growth	Leader is benefited in all related ways. (Presumably he shares the honors.)	Leader strives for growth in all members of the group.
5. Rewards	Leader flourishes. (Associates low paid as common practice, but not necessarily so.)	All share rewards and choose sacrifices.
6. Models	Some of the potentates of history, or industrialists like Henry Ford are models.	Jesus, George Washington, Lincoln are models.
7. Defense	People defend leader.	Leader defends people
8. Attitude	Inflexible.	Flexible
9. Methods	Gives jobs to men. (Personality oriented.) Must command.	Gives men to jobs. (Task oriented.) Must inspire.
10. Loyalty	Loyalty is to leader. (Joab to David.)	Loyalty is to purpose. (Paul and Barnabas.)

Autocratic leader vs. person leader [cont'd]

	Autocratic Leader	Person Leader
11. Salary	Determined by what the market will bear—labor is a purchasable product.	Determined by what is fair—labor is people. (What is the institution able to pay?)
12. Competency	Personal.	Professional.
13. Evaluation	Irrelevant because of subjective orientation.	Relevant because of objective orientation.
14. Abilities	Adapts to own weaknesses to protect image.	Adapts to strengths—using skills in others wherever they may be found.
15. Strength	Ownership.	Skill.
16. Discipline	Regimented quality.	Self-discipline quality.
17. Exploitation	For the leader.	For the agreed-upon purpose.
18. Risk	High for leader so postpone until certain of results.	Equal for all so all are honored or all are blamed.
19. Vision	"I see the leader." "I just work here."	"I see the cause." "I belong here."
20. Status	Diminished for followers. (Workers.) Central authority.	Enhanced for followers. (Workers.) Diffused authority.
21. Tasks	Overlapping and unclear.	Orientation and description.

It is easy to identify preferences for the person leader. In a democratic society the humane nature of person-oriented followers and leaders makes the autocratic leader appear anachronistic. Democratic processes do not assure effectiveness. Leaders may not be exclusively categorized, nor is the effectiveness of any leadership guaranteed. Followers are also mixed in their characteristics, responding favorably to those leader types they prefer.

Both leader types listed above have succeeded, both failed, in various circumstances. The characterizations do not fit every case. Some leaders seem to move back and forth. One might make a case for Jesus as an autocratic leader in circumstances requiring authority, especially when followers flagged. If Jesus were physically present in our time a committed Christian would likely be willing to invite Jesus to total and unquestioned leadership.

Descriptions of company leaders and authority figures are circulated in literature from time to time. During 1977 a study showed that such a person begins his career in his twenties. He holds a college degree in business. He remains with a single employer for thirty years or more and devotes 60 hours a week to company business. Midwesterners who seem to enjoy work as much as leisure appear to be gratified and are evaluated as the most effective among their peers. They commonly make one or two speeches a month. The largest problems they faced in 1977 were government regulations, inflation, energy shortage, competition for capital and union demands.*

The Scriptures stipulate or imply that many issues of leadership are the same or similar in sacred as well as secular situations. The differences are, in general, spiritual ones. For Christian leadership such issues as vision, maturity, integrity, spiritual knowledge, balance (wholeness), discipling, and love are vital. For secularists these points are uneven in importance. We acknowledge

---

* "What It Takes To Run a Big Company," **U.S. News and World Report**, Dec. 12, 1977, p. 69.

disagreement and confusion for critics at both levels of perception. For both viewpoints there is large agreement on ethical motivation, goal orientation, practical applications, problem solving, futuristic considerations, communications, evaluations, and use of time. Whatever is done, by whatever style of leadership, the ultimate purpose is, or ought to be, effectiveness in meeting the needs of persons as individuals and, collectively, as society.

LEADERSHIP GENERATES
SUCCESS THROUGH STRESS

A leader may expect to encounter personal and interpersonal barriers as he works to carry through his task. He is sometimes at odds with himself, his purposes, and people. Each of these can be in competition with the others. Although each factor in its rightful balance with others is supposed to contribute to leadership, each also possesses its own dynamics. When it is segregated from everything else, it is different. This makes analysis difficult, sometimes impossible.

Contradictions commonly create stress. What happens when an individual is in contradiction with himself? Wise leaders know they will not always wish to lead, but they also know that to suspend their efforts, even temporarily, may mean loss of everything. There are always others who wish to fill a vacuum, or perceived vacuum. A substitution might lose everything. Followers are not willing to shift so easily. They do not like to be abandoned. A leader cannot move in and out of duty as he can move assignments and people.

Although most people acknowledge great need for leadership, they also are suspicious of it, even fear it. Camus wrote, in a poem, that he did not desire a leader for he might not wish to follow; nor did he wish to lead; so he would have all persons walk side by side as companions. It is an appealing perception even if unrealistic. Much in life cannot be done without leaders and followers. Most persons experience shifting attitudes and loyalties in following anyone. The success or failure of their leaders has much to do with the shift.

Followers are quick to ascribe failure to their leaders. They may, by their neutrality, aid failure. But they may also be caught up by the dynamics of a leader's charisma, and follow that leader without evaluating related situations. They may follow when they ought not to do so. To follow or not to follow is the question, and each ought to possess its own legitimate reasons.

Purposes are necessary to leadership. They give it direction. However, they can create problems on their own requiring intermediate solutions, because they too are dynamic. There are always dynamics to be encountered and not all of them can be anticipated. Purposes grow, shift, change. So do times, weather, economies. Life and death matters change plans. Both leaders and followers may not be flexible enough to make adjustments. They like matters to be clear at the outset and remain static through to the end. Followers are often offended by dynamics and withdraw. A leader may see that a project will be different from what it was at the outset because of shifts and changes in circumstances. Even persons involved in the venture enter and leave to create some of the problems. In such instances the leader adapts. He does the best he can in these changing circumstances.

In this competition of stress-creating forces, a prevailing leader must have stamina. Stamina is not merely energy or lasting physical and mental capacities. It is enough of the perception of "youth" that permits one to take risks. Those who feel "old" feel they have done their part. They have paid their "dues." They should not, they believe, be called upon to do more. Having suffered the blows of life, they become defensive. They have known, in Shakespeare's words, "the slings and arrows of outrageous fortune." Why go through them again?

A remarkable illustration of leadership, from the inception of an idea to the end of the project, appears in the experience of Nehemiah. Although a Jew, he had risen to a position of high servanthood to the pagan king as cupbearer, an assignment which gave him status and some leisure. Even though a new generation in Israel had appeared following the captivity under Nebuchadnezzar, Nehemiah and others maintained their faith and hope for their people and homeland. Receiving news of the continued devastation of Jerusalem, Nehemiah was taken with grief. In deep stress, he wept and mourned about what he had heard. He fasted and prayed about his concern (Neh. 1).

During ensuing weeks, the personal regimen exacted a physical toll on Nehemiah. The strain became obvious so that even the king remarked about it. Nehemiah explained the circumstances of his homeland. As is so often the case in worthy causes, when persons possessing resources are apprised, the king offered assistance. Strained concern turned to relief for Nehemiah (Neh. 2).

Nehemiah conceived a plan to rebuild Jerusalem. He would be given letters from the king to the governors to assure the passage of Nehemiah's party, and a letter to provide timber building materials. The king, satisfied with Nehemiah's time schedule, released him for the project and provided military escort. However, another cause for stress arose from external forces. Arriving in the area, Nehemiah was immediately faced with resistance from the local officials, who chose not to honor the letters. The officials were firm in resisting Jewish restoration.

Nehemiah, personally confident, prepared himself for this resistance. Alone, he evaluated the circumstances, inspected the premises by night, and formed a plan. Presenting his case and plan convincingly, Nehemiah inspired the workers: "Let us arise and build. So they put their hands to the good work" (Neh. 2:18). Nevertheless, resistance continued. With tenacity Nehemiah articulated his commission. Even with resistance the work advanced (Neh. 3). Nehemiah adapted well to stress.

LEADERSHIP GENERATES
SUCCESS THROUGH STRENGTH

What are some of the traits of an effective leader that reveal his strength? As already suggested, a clear list of attributes is elusive. What is taken as a trait relating to strength in one context may later be less helpful. For example, charisma is a cyclical trait, becoming impressive in one generation and taken as not only unimportant but a negative factor in another. Mayor Richard Daley of Chicago was perceived to be a charismatic leader by a significant percentage of the electorate of the city. He did many things, surviving political wars that would destroy other leaders. Franklin Roosevelt and John Kennedy exuded charisma and were followed by the electorate, in part, for that reason. Lyndon Johnson, perceived by the eastern establishment as being without charisma, was denied latitudes granted to Kennedy. As a rule, there must be a time lapse before charismatic leaders, as currently accepted, may be objectively evaluated. There is no evidence that charisma is necessary to leadership. Charisma is pleasant, sometimes expected by followers, and seems to help the leader along. But many leaders do well without it.

Nearly every characteristic of a leader must be related to relevant features for impact. All require interpretation. Goodness and virtue become examples in point. Goodness for one culture may be evil in another. Confucius is virtually deified for his ethics. So is Mao, but for differing, even opposing, ethics. The force of Mao's leadership was in the revolution of his country. Some people believed, and some continue to believe, that Mao was virtually a political holy man. But he, by that "holiness," could order murders. Ghandi's greatest strength was his perceived virtue, found in peace, not murder, in pacifism, not war. He denied himself in various ways, following lengthy fasts, meditating and even taking a vow of celibacy. His leadership was magnificent before a colonial power committed to democracy. With the Nazis and Hitler, Ghandi would have been obliterated, as many pacific men were obliterated by Hitler's troops.

Popes and priests of the Catholic Church exude a type of leadership through their reputations as celibate men whose lives are totally devoted to the Church. A perception of virtue is major in their authority with followers. Nevertheless, neither these men, nor others, can rely solely on virtue to lead their people. Their enemies and persons holding other basic views may not accept them as virtuous. Virtue, in such instances, is in the eye of the beholder. For the Christian it is the meeting of biblical standards.

In Christianity virtue as it is defined by Scripture is highly regarded, and in some religious bodies leadership fails when the leader loses perceived virtue. But virtue, so highly regarded, does not a leader make. Nor does an evil man lose his ability to lead unless he is destroyed by his evil. It appears that Saul, the king, was doomed when his evil drove him into schizophrenia. Jezebel, Ahab, and Herod victimized themselves through their evil, their lack of virtue. Hitler and Mussolini were their own worst enemies. Ruling for more than four decades before the birth of Jesus, Herod was "great," and is called Great in history, but his skills as a leader, like those of Hitler, were diluted, then lost as he sank into his depravity.

The evangelical church, committed as it is to biblical concepts, must retain value virtues in its leadership. These are taught in principle (2 Pet. 1). Anyone can verify them in the repetition of textual illustrations. Men, like David, suffered over their loss of righteousness, and their leadership was challenged when they sinned. David's leadership was, in part, related to modeling virtues to the people. When he declined as a model, his leadership waned.

Another strength factor is the personal security and stability in a leader, making him competent to withstand caustic accusations and criticisms. Some of what is said about him and sometimes to him is untrue and unfair. He is neither destroyed by these attacks nor does he waste time defending himself extensively. As already noted, he does not dignify some statements by answering them.

The leader senses cleavage, even if slight, between himself and the outer world. The feeling is almost invariable. Part of this differential is forced on him because of the natural break that occurs between those who lead and those who follow that leadership. It may be necessary to keep leadership within appropriate limits. Even so, the tendency to isolate himself can lead to destructiveness in some leaders. Too threatened by separation, the leader may feel sorry for himself, read signs incorrectly, fall into self-doubt or become intolerant. He can become self-destructive if the issues are large enough and he is infirm about himself. He must be a man of strength to evade these dangers.

LEADERSHIP GENERATES SUCCESS THROUGH STRATEGY

The tools of leadership are personality, character, position and competence. The question arises as to how these tools are to be used. Each includes positive and negative characteristics. Leadership, in the way we wish to perceive leadership, accents positive values: manipulation follows negative.

Personality is sometimes a mystery. We are told that personality is sufficiently understandable that it can be guided into change either for improvement or decline. Even so, we become aware of personality differences in children before anyone has made conscious effort to affect their personalities. Some enjoy personalities that win favorable attention from other children and adults. They seem physically attractive, somewhat ahead of their peers in social graces and acceptance, and destined to win advantage. They receive the teacher's attention and best remarks, they get the best date, identifying with a special "in" group, and they are elected to offices in student organizations.

In adult life, if their advantages remain, these people seem to flourish if they also have style, and some wealth or feature by which they effectively reflect themselves. If Herbert Hoover had emanated personality as Franklin Roosevelt did during depression years, he might have survived politically in the economic disaster of world depression. Roosevelt, after two terms as president of the United States, did not bring the nation out of depression. It took a world war to do that. But he did create an attitude generally interpreted as beneficial to the people. He tried to do something. When what he tried did not work, or was rejected, he tried something else. He exuded an energy, a style, a personality that animated the populace. Some of his programs were Hoover's, but advanced with a flair, an air of confidence.

More recently in history, John Fitzgerald Kennedy provided personality and style to his campaign for the presidency and the manner in which he functioned in office. After his tragic death, the personality change perceived in Lyndon Baines Johnson and Richard M.

Nixon made the efforts of these men less attractive to Americans. Kennedy was forgiven weaknesses, and some were not even mentioned by media or analysts, because he had style and personality in his person and family. He was a liberal patrician coming down to the people. Johnson seemed like a Texas rancher trying to become a patrician. Or he was a rancher among many patricians. He was criticized for carrying through some of the policies begun by his predecessor.

Anyone acquainted with Christian work can fairly well predict patterns that will likely emerge in ministries. Often there is an "image" looked for in a minister. Scores of large and influential churches are pastored by men who fit personality molds acceptable to the various church or community bodies. A minister with the preferred personality and style, even physical appearance, is virtually assured of a fine invitation and appointment. Surely there is a danger here to stereotype when there is described the "Presbyterian" or "Baptist" or "Methodist" style and personality; but there is a difference, and that difference means much in the various denominations. Sometimes it is not consciously perceived and applied, but it is there.

Personality is an element of ethos. It helps people want to do what the persuader says ought to be done. But personality, when it is attractive, may well be a disadvantage in that the leader may rely too heavily upon it. He does not do his homework. He fails to bring substance to his professional development. He perceives his power in himself, and will ultimately fail unless he completes larger plans and purposes.

Biblical characters who appear to have possessed attractive personalities are Abraham, David, Absalom, Samson, Solomon, Andrew, Peter, John, Barnabas, among others. Men like Saul and other kings in the Old Testament and the apostle Paul in the New seem to have wrestled with personality problems. Saul changed negatively in personality, and Paul positively. Timothy appears to have developed in personality from the time of his early ministry to latter.

Character has often been included as a topic for leadership. But character means different things to different people, and varies between cultures. In American and Canadian history character has been closely related to personal righteousness and Judaeo-Christian values, especially as they were interpreted by white, Anglo-Saxon Protestanism. In 1928 Alfred Smith, a Catholic, could not be elected president of the United States partly because of the electorate's continuing concern accented in the nineteenth century as "rum and Romanism." Adlai Stevenson could not be elected in 1952 or 1956 partly because he was a divorced man. Kennedy, elected in 1960, was Catholic. Ronald Reagan, elected in 1980, was divorced and remarried. Apparently a majority of Americans in the last decades of the twentieth century did not relate character to deviation from Protestantism or marriage solidarity. In Canada, Prime Minister Pierre Trudeau was elected and reelected even though his wife was involved in scandal, and he was the object of her vituperative public statements.

During recent decades, character evaluation has generally shifted from personal to corporate perceptions. Character is more and more measured by how one feels and acts in congress with others in concern for poverty, in the protection of wildlife and resources, in the efforts for peace in the world, in the struggle for human rights and equality. In this way a person may have unsatisfactory personal habits and weaknesses, but be perceived as high in social character because of concern for society.

During recent years college administrations have found that many students tolerate in themselves and others considerable latitude in language, fidelity, honesty and personal habits, but have tightened their expectations for the performance of institutions. In former times, institutions were permitted failure they are not permitted today. I have worked with students morally and ethically in violation of both religious and civil codes, but who were impeccable in their beliefs about how nations, churches, schools and businesses ought to function. This view of corporate character appears to have prevailed in the closing decades of the twentieth century. Some candidates with personal morals that might have sent them to jail in an earlier generation are elected to office because of their perceived social morality. One might rewrite Reinhold Niebuhr's most eminent title from "Moral Man and Immoral Society" to "Immoral Man and Moral Society."

Many church leaders have taken the social position. Some ministers have been married, divorced and remarried. The use of alcohol and mild drugs is not unusual in some denominational circles formerly prohibitionist. Sexual dalliance, if it is sufficiently discreet, is not cause for losing position in some groups. Even homosexuality is accepted in several denominations, and criticisms of the practice of homosexuality is sometimes represented as un-Christian. Some openly acknowledged homosexuals have received ordination in the first-line denominations.

The point to be made is that, at the time of this writing, personal character is not interpreted as once it was, and the former standard appears to be less important to leadership. Even so, a very large part of society, especially in the evangelical culture, holds to beliefs in personal character for leaders as it is defined in practical biblical terms.

It is commonly believed that in the church the more one hears about personal character and its relationship to Christian life, the less he will hear about social character.

Among evangelicals there is a basic assumption at work, that raising the level of personal character in enough persons will raise the social character of the community. It is also believed that unless personal character is improved, social change will not move upward for long. It may very well be that the American attempt begun with Franklin Roosevelt and escalated with the efforts of Lyndon Johnson, to meet the needs of citizens through compassionate government, may be a case in point. When government tried to provide for the truly needy, a mass of freeloaders eventually emerged. Government, expanding in elephantine proportions, was neither flexible enough nor affluent enough to meet all issues related to social problem solving. Government became too costly. Its management was too bureaucratic to be efficient. And no one knows how to run things in government without bureaucracy.

Social character in church leadership has strengthened. Evangelical leaders argue for voluntary participation in meeting world needs, like hunger. They use the electronic media to tell their stories. In the name of Christ these people write books and articles on social issues. They design programs to feed the poor, especially deprived children in foreign lands. They are interested in refugees. They develop political action groups and lobby governments for improvements in conditions. Increasingly, they use available social structures to achieve their purposes. They learn from others. The Moral Majority, which attracted a large number of evangelicals, was motivated by a cause as were Americans for Democratic Action, the American Civil Liberties Union, and the National Association for the Advancement of Colored People. Each has, or had, a cause to represent. Each attracted resistance as well as support. Each had a right to birth in a democratic society.

The point to be made here is that the leader has a

strategy of personal character, and of *a character relating to the cause that serves his followers*. He must be perceived as consistent in that character classification and he must monitor it for change. Change or fluctuation will surely occur. When Daniel Webster missed that point in the emerging social character of his time, he was nearly destroyed. When the poet John Greenleaf Whittier heard that Webster acknowledged slaves as property, a legal fact at the time, he wrote "Ichabod." Once taken as socially acceptable, even if unpalatable, slavery lost that acceptability. Rather it became a sign of immorality, both personal and social. That slaves were property by law was no longer acceptable, no longer normal.

Position is important because a leader must have earned, been appointed, inherited, seized, or in some way achieved an influential status. This matter is dealt with elsewhere in this writing but must be inserted in any list of strategy tools. When a leader is in a place of authority and knows it, he has leverage that can be utilized in doing things or getting things done. Authority comes from various sources, but position is one major factor. It makes leadership easier, if the leader has it. If position is the only source of leadership power, then the leader must have it. Leadership must always relate to power, of some kind.

Leadership implies role fulfillment. A king is expected to act like a king, a president like a president, a manager like a manager, a general like a general, a minister like a minister, a father like a father. Leadership is partly the fulfillment of a particular role. President Jimmy Carter lost some of the force of his office by trying to maintain his image as an ordinary citizen. He spoke softly, carried his own garment bag from planes, wore sweaters instead of suit jackets, and generally carried himself comfortably. Many Americans were uncomfortable calling their president "Jimmy." The aura relating to high position was missing. (On the other hand, he also began a style of casualness that would permit presidents after him to be less formal.)

One must handle authority with humility and care, but he must use that authority without apology. Authority is somewhere in the nature of things. Those who, in the name of democracy, would excessively weaken authority will end with neither democracy nor problem solving. There is the problem of insouciance, common to history, which is the periodical abdication of responsibility and decision.

Authority is not autocracy. It requires checks and balances. It does not invest the leader with divine right. The leader does carry duty and must assume responsibility for what he does. In this responsibility, according to the Scriptures, he has some defense in doing God's service.

Competency is the fourth tool. A leader ought to evaluate his competency to serve. Personality, character, even position are not enough. Many fine leaders have served without personality features that would have assisted them. They might choose, as Moses did Aaron and Hobab, assistants who were effective in interpersonal relations. Moreover, many leaders have achieved greatness without character: Ahab, Herod, Hitler, Catherine of Russia. Each had to develop means for holding their followers. Hitler's means was partly embodied in his prejudice about Aryan superiority. He publicized a theoretical character to those who might benefit from it. And although position is a major tool for leadership, it is not the ultimate one. Position is power, but the leader must utilize power centers or theories and exploit them for specific purposes. This action requires high competency.

In the end, the matter of leadership turns on competency. Either the leader is in himself competent, or is competent to put effective personnel in places of leadership. Competency is, basically, the ability to do what ought to be done through people. The measure of history has been at the point of competency. That is where the victory is won.

God's measure begins with love, faith, righteousness. His economy is of a different sort than that of the world. That devout men and women put His value system first in importance does not diminish or displace competency or other factors listed above as keys to leadership. All persons could and should love their fellow man, could have faith, could grow in righteousness. But not all persons are competent to accomplish significant purposes. To possess Christian virtues does not make the devout man a leader except as his life models character for others to follow. But the problems are more far ranging than character alone can solve.

It appears that God bypasses even His followers to permit competent men to lead. Cyrus was called to purpose before he had any clear idea about a relationship to a personal God. And the apostle Paul acknowledged a pagan Caesar to believers in presenting a theory of government in Romans 13. Even Jesus gave Caesar his due, paying His taxes. Students of history do not find Christians to have been more competent at government than non-Christians. The promise of leadership in a person is in his competency for managing persons and things. We might hope that the leader is also one of Christian character, as the Scriptures define character. However, we remember that character, without competency at leadership, even though it provides a valuable model for good, may not be sufficient for our purpose here.

We return to our observations of Nehemiah as a leader. Bible readers must be impresed with Nehemiah's strategy and methods. Nehemiah knew his purpose; he knew the situation, having taken careful inventory of circumstances; he had a plan; he was articulate to state his case and confront his detractors; and, he was well acquainted with the names of the workers and their assignments (Neh. 3).

Nehemiah treated personal abuse and put-down in a prayerful response that undoubtedly fortified his spirit and prevented him from wasting energy in fruitless exchanges that would further infuriate his enemies. The work proceeded with quality control. Security measures were taken both to protect the completed work and to permit laborers to continue their work. When his own people were fearful, he persuaded them to maintain their procedures. And they did (Neh. 4).

When, with some success, the Jewish people began to settle in their land, a drouth introduced an unexpected problem. Persons redeemed from slavery and captivity were being resold, even to fellow Jews, in order to meet the exigency. Again Nehemiah, after analyzing the problems, called upon his considerable rhetorical skill to stop the practice. His persuasion was dramatically successful (Neh. 5:1-3).

So effective was Nehemiah that he was appointed governor in Judah. So excellent was he in administration that, during the period he was governor, the people provided for themselves without welfare from the king, although allowance was available. It was Nehemiah's policy to make the people free "because of the fear of God." His predecessors had burdened the people and exacted more than just tribute from them. Further, Nehemiah maintained close communion with leaders serving under him, and with regularity provided personal rewards, principally in food and drink. Nehemiah did what he did with conscious effort, knowing leadership was needed that he could provide. He hoped for reward for his efforts. He acknowledged that he worked hard and expressed desire that God might remember him for the job well done (Neh. 5:14-49).

Nehemiah, like other leaders, was threatened by his enemies. Plots appeared to remove Nehemiah either through death or fear. He demonstrated his sophistication as a leader by refusing fear, and making a case through astute use of letters and embassies. There can be no doubt that his faith and prayerful treatment of problems maintained him when he might have wavered. His commitment and resoluteness appear to have held weaker leaders and followers in the restoration program (Neh. 6).

Nehemiah consolidated his position, making sure that his lieutenants were, like himself, committed to spiritual ideals. Census and resources were listed (Neh. 7). Religious life was restored to the people, and a constitution was ordered as a covenant to which representative signatories committed themselves. Fundamental in his interpretation of God's instructions to Israel, in Nehemiah's view, was purity. Although strict in carrying through the theocratic elements of the restoration, Nehemiah yearned for the freedom of his people, and defied those in or out of Israel who would mistreat them through slavery, inflation, or dependence upon the state (Neh. 7-13).

That Nehemiah was a success is a matter of history. His motivation was to please God, and the work he did he meant to be to the glory of God. Through his investment he expected to be rewarded at God's pleasure.

Few, if any, Bible narratives on a particular subject are so complete or succinct as the story of supreme human leadership modeled in Nehemiah.

—7—

The Progeny of Leadership
FOLLOWERS

And he said to them, Follow me, and I will make you fishers of men.

—Matthew 4:19

Verily, verily, I say unto you, He that entereth not by the door into the sheepfold, but climbeth up some other way, the same is a thief and a robber. But he that entereth in by the door is the shepherd of the sheep. To him the porter openeth; and the sheep hear his voice: and he calleth his own sheep by name, and leadeth them out. And when he putteth forth his own sheep, he goeth before them, and the sheep follow him: for they know his voice. And a stranger will they not follow, but will flee from him: for they know not the voice of strangers.

—John 10:1-5

Jesus said to candidate followers, prospective disciples, "Come, follow me." Later, the apostle Paul wrote: "Be ye followers of me, as I am of Christ." Following appears to be vital, not merely for the honor of the leader, but for the benefit of followers and to the success of some mutual venture.

Jesus taught His disciples about leadership/followership in several passages preserved for us. In John's Gospel, chapter 10, there are accents upon certain leadership attributes: genuineness, identity, sensitivity, knowledge, self-risking and vision making. Jesus also clarifies some basic attributes of followers. They settle on their leader and become loyal to him. The appeals of other leaders are like appeals from thieves and robbers. Followers, knowing their needs, choose a sensible, orderly way. Any other way is like avoiding the door and climbing stealthily over the wall. Followers make their decisions, believing or knowing what their leader is like. They trust him. Followers have a vested interest in the cause, together with their leader. The false leader, like a transient hireling, possesses no lasting future for himself in the event, so abandons his duty. Followers who are wise know that. Genuineness of motives in a follower may be seen in his choices of leadership. Followers seek leaders who use the door, the planned way, rather than taking some other access, an unnatural way.

There is little doubt that the masses are greatly

disappointed and disillusioned with many persons occupying places of leadership. By 1980, after several disappointing decades in American history, doubt about leaders created an inevitable apathy in the population. Erosion of public confidence in leaders means that confidence will erode in institutions, as various polls have indicated. During the mid-1960s, 76 percent of Americans trusted their government. By the mid-1970s, and following Watergate, the figure dropped to 33 percent. More than 80 percent said they did not trust government as much as formerly. There was a ripple effect on others. Professionals, representing many fields, also lost the confidence of the public.

Trust in leadership does break down when events conspire to break it down. Unloving critics have increased public disappointment and disillusionment. And, it must be acknowledged, promises from leaders have been broken more often than one would expect them to be. People must see leadership results close to their experiences to maintain confidence. Elected officials soon learn that fact.

THE NATURE OF FOLLOWERS

How does one identify an effective follower? There are a number of traits that have been identified. One study shows that a follower: a) is willing to be led, b) values human life, c) is sexually stable, d) believes in utilizing resources, e) is personally honest and, f) defends the right to own property.

Leadership assumes that there are persons willing to be led, persons who believe in others. They have the ability to sublimate themselves in some way for the achievement of purpose. They own appropriate humility and trust. Some analysts believe distrust is the greatest threat related to followership effectiveness.

Serious followers value human life. Fine soldiers are obedient to their commanders because they know that following orders in battle will likely save more lives than would be the case if each man is his own leader. Followers valuing human life tend to keep laws. Observing laws, they expect to avoid accidents, avoid crime, avoid disorder. They hope for a quality of life. They cooperate to preserve both quality life and life itself.

In seeking to identify significant traits of an effective follower, researchers held no inkling in advance that one trait would be sexual stability. Deviates, exotics, intemperate persons do not generally follow well. They cannot be counted on at standard levels. They are commonly taken with their own preoccupation to the degree they have little to give, or little they wish to give, to the cause. Institutions are rightly concerned about the sexual stability of both leaders and followers, but the issue is more basic and relevant for followers than leaders. A follower distracted from standard family roles commonly weakens his commitments to leaders. In contrast, a leader, while he will possess many other positive characteristics, may not possess the features of a good follower. He may be less stable sexually than his followers. As a rule he hides that instability. It may cost him his leadership. But he takes privilege; he feels he has discretionary resources available to him. He feels he deserves perquisites.

Followers believe in utilizing resources. This is not to say they are prodigal in that use. They know progress is related to putting things and people to work for worthy purposes. There is no need to lead or follow if something is not used up in the doing. What is used, worn out, or destroyed provides something in return worth the investment. Persons who do not use resources, or find that they do not wish to do so, are not likely going to follow a leader. The leader will not want them because they will not contribute to progress. Social dropouts generally do not perceive that the earth is a natural resource to be used in appropriate ways.

Commonly, followers are strong in favoring personal honesty. The concept of high personal character may be stronger for a community of followers. They have a fairly well-developed sense of justice and right. When all is in place, and activity begins, followers believe the workings should be oiled by honest dealings. They hope for equity. They are willing to work for what they presume is equity.

Owning property, like sexual stability, turned out to be a surprise in this follower list of characteristics. Dedicated followers tend to believe that ownership has something to do with cause to follow leadership. Again, underlying belief in order and equity seems to hold the effective follower. Perhaps the whole matter of commitment is related to a belief that something tangible can be protected, claimed, transferred. Communist countries find that efficiency increases when workers on commune farms are given their own plot of ground. Factory production declines as workers perceive that the business is owned by the state even if held in the name of the people. They would likely follow their leaders better if the plant were privately owned, or truly owned by the workers. State ownership seems least effective of the options.

THE DIFFERENCES IN FOLLOWERS

A leader, at the highest level and treating the most important human problems, knows he confronts virtually impossible situations. He knows there are no true or total solutions available to him. The depravity of man guarantees that, at very best, there are only alternatives with some better than others, but none perfect. The best leader identifies the best option and seeks its adoption.

Whatever the major problems are among men, they cannot be ended. Moses may accomplish great things, but Israel will decline in faith. Samuel, David and Solomon, and other kings after them, will recall the people, but decline will follow. Elijah will win the day, but captivity will come. Ezra and Nehemiah will see restoration, but Rome will prevail. And so the story repeats itself in the history of man. The peace to end all wars, following World War I, is followed by World War II. The search for peace by leaders in our time is presumed to be delay so that war will not occur in the generation those leaders represent. They hope for little more than respite. A long respite might bypass a war or two, or the ferocity of a war might be, for a time, reduced. Leaders would do more if they could, but the nature of things limits their accomplishments. The best leader guides his followers into the best available options.

Leaders must bear the burden of accusation that they seldom settle things. The best they can do, if permitted to do their best, is to create tolerable conditions. Even those tolerable conditions will become unsatisfactory and demand solution. Israel "groaned" under slavery in Egypt. Led into the wilderness by Moses, they are fed with "manna," tolerable fare if deliverance from slavery is remembered. But manna becomes a bore: "there is nothing but this manna before our eyes." The people remembered the fleshpots of Egypt, "the melons, the leeks, the onions, and the garlic." Egyptian slavery is forgotten. The solution to slavery, release in the wilderness and simple fare, now becomes the problem.

Much of the narrative of the Pentateuch, Joshua and Judges concerns itself with the tension between leaders and followers. The exchanges between Moses and the people, between Moses and Aaron and the people, may suggest more to the reader about shifts in the strength of followership than leadership. The tragic events that kept

Israel in the wilderness forty years, and the events occurring during that period, as well as later in establishing the kingdom, seem more to have been failures of followership than leadership. Moses was good at his job and getting better all the time. Joshua was equal to the task. Many later judges were excellent.

When Moses flinched in leadership, it was generally the consequence of anger. He, when angry, smashed things. Smiting the rock when he was bidden to speak, was the act that forfeited his entry into the promised land. Nevertheless, Moses was an outstanding leader. Nothing can dim the record of a man who broke the power of slavery for a nation of one million people, who gained their release, who led them as vulnerable as they were in a wilderness, avoiding extensive military engagement, who gave them a law operative more than three thousand years after it was delivered, who bound the people together in one language and faith, who brought them to the gate of the land they would conquer for their own, and who ordained another leader to accomplish the final goal of conquest. Israel lives in the shadow of Moses even today.

Followers of Moses offered large volumes of resistance. The circumstances in Egypt, the dangers along the way, the refusal of some, like Achan, to follow, and the periodic rebellion of the people, suggest that the larger problem was followership. Given the circumstances (the on-again/off-again people, the flagging of their faith when a land could have been taken, the hankering of the people for a more visible religion, and even the loss of his personal family support), Moses might well have abandoned this venture and initiated another.

The biblical concept of following includes at least three large meanings. To follow means to *cling to a leader*. It is assumed that the follower has found a leader worth the loyalty. A follower *may be an imitator* in replicating a leader's words and ways. Imitation is matching, even emulating, the person and work of worth. By imitation, ancients presumed to learn how to do things well. In this educative technique the model might be surpassed. Ancient speakers sought to emulate Demosthenes or Cicero. Christians are urged to follow in the model system with Christ the lead Model.

Finally, a follower *is in active pursuit of the leader's wishes*. This is not only to be like the leader, but to carry out the plan and program he proposes. In Christianity all three perceptions well apply—to cling to the leader, to imitate him, and to follow diligently his program.

THE RESULTS FOR FOLLOWERS

Why does followership fail? There are a number of reasons, and we do not presume to identify all factors. Perhaps the leading one is found in the weakness of human nature. Society seems to have become unrealistic about human nature even though the idealism about it was long ago dealt severe blows, any one of which might be unto death. Early in the twentieth century the aphorism was popular: "Every day in every way we are getting better and better." Following two horrible world wars and a few lesser ones, massive depression, enormous crime rates, and scores of other evidences, one is hard put to espouse the perfectability of man. But the illusion dies hard. More, much more, is expected of man than man is giving, perhaps than he can give. Even more is expected of leaders. No one produces sufficiently well to meet these unrealistic expectations. Leadership and followership fail more often simply because human beings fail in normal course.

Rising expectations create a basic problem. Psychologists warn individuals not to raise expectations excessively. If they do, they tend to give up. Achievement may fall below what it would be if expectations were lower, but realistic, so as to stimulate hope for success. When the goal is possible, we are more likely to try for it than if it is perceived to be too far above us, beyond our potential. When unrealistic expectations are held out for others, even small groups, the likelihood of disappointment is great. We seem never to be more openly disappointed than when we are disappointed in others. This is basic to cynicism, a widespread problem among adults.

Followers may be thwarted when success does not appear as early as they expect it to occur. If an effort is slowed or temporarily halted, many followers give up. Their commitments may have been low at the outset. Seasoned leaders know that new problems and periodic stalls unduly discourage some followers. Jesus' experience with the 120 disciples well illustrates the point. Returning after their first two-by-two missionary journeys, this larger circle of disciples was ecstatic. These unnamed disciples were pleased with the response they experienced. Jesus then recited sacrifices He would require for future effective ministry. With that information some members of the group filtered away. They, like we commonly do, related effective leadership to success as society measures success. Work would receive a measurable reward in short order. Jesus did not relate to that perception.

The Scriptures provide insight on failure of followership. When, from his headquarters in Rome, the apostle Paul gained mixed response from auditors on his gospel message, he reminded the people about the Isaiah passage on rejection:

> You will keep on hearing, but will not understand:
> And you will keep on seeing, but will not perceive;
> For the heart of this people has become dull,
> And with their ears they scarcely hear,
> And they have closed their eyes;

> Lest they should see with their eyes,
> And hear with their ears,
> And understand with their heart and return,
> And I should heal them.
>
> (Acts 28:26b-27)

Just as some followers drop projects because the effort required exceeds their willingness to invest themselves, so some will resign because too little is required. They atrophy when they are not used. If nothing happens within a reasonable period of time, if the leader lags in a manner that seems to slow any progress, dynamic followers may be expected to slow down, then cease activity. They will defect to someone else, or, if comfortable with reduction in effort, they commonly shift to "no interest." The loss of motivation makes them different people.

Another reason for failure of followers is traceable to misunderstanding of institutions. Institutions, created by imperfect men, are themselves imperfect. They are born, grow, mature, fade and die, unless something is done to renew them. This is essentially the theory of Arnold Toynbee in his story of governments. Institutions cannot return to their people more than is invested in them. No government can distribute to its people more than the people vest in it. No church can do more than ministers and parishioners are willing to do.

The basic belief in institutions is that persons can do together, in cooperative ventures, what they cannot do as individuals. The smallest institution, the family, is a protective device, comforting and nurturing its members. A business enterprise provides a service or product an individual could not likely provide at a reasonable cost.

The results of leadership/followership seem obvious. Where leadership is exercised in a family there is order, solidarity, security. The family holds together. It is a basic principle in the description of the Christian family (Eph. 5).

Where leadership holds in a corporation, the direction for personnel, the quality of the product, the planning, the marketing, and all that goes into the business may be expected to help the followers. Little of what the affluent nations possess could be gained without leadership. Starvation rises where leadership and management are in short supply. People are more likely to starve because leadership is not available to manage resources than because food is unavailable.

Where leadership mobilizes followers to accomplish national purposes, nearly anything within reason can be done. With great national goals publicized, citizens would be called upon to carry well-defined responsibilities. If resources are dedicated for the common good in this leadership/followership, history will ascribe greatness and general satisfaction to the society.

Where similar principles are applied in a church setting, there are high expectations. Presumably, with divine assistance, things can be done largely, but also "decently and in order." Followers respecting the basic principles of Scriptures, find that guidelines are clear. The purpose of world evangelism is first work, the worship of God is first privilege, and obedience is first duty. The spiritual leadership/followership that advances those priority matters is of great concern for the church. If followers will align themselves with leaders who seek the completion of Christian mission, the results will carry eternal meaning.

No leader is effective to the degree we would like for him to be. But there are features we may find gratifying, sufficiently so that we can place confidence in some leaders. In doing so we become effective followers. Perhaps the lines between leaders and followers are more difficult to draw than we have believed. Charles A.

Garfield carefully interviewed 250 high achievers, persons from whom leadership might be expected. The ten most distinct characteristics in the high achievers, setting them apart from less productive, may provide clues for identifying leaders who are highly effective from those who might be less effective. And we might find information about followers who are highly effective from those who are low in participation or ineffective in participation.

Garfield's characteristics, adjusted somewhat here for our purposes and structure, of high achievers include: 1) Foresight, and that foresight incorporates ability to carry through planning strategies; 2) Accomplishment, and that accomplishment incorporates transcending previous levels of their own accomplishments; 3) Self, and that self incorporates improving levels of confidence and worth; 4) Responsibility, and that responsibility incorporates a need to control in order to carry out duty; 5) Communication, and that communication skill incorporates salesmanship ability; 6) Rehearsal, and that rehearsal incorporates intellectual treatment, in advance, for critical incidents and key situations; 7) Fulfillment, and that fulfillment incorporates the work in such a way that there is little need for praise or recognition; 8) Risk, and that risk incorporates a superior ability in taking creative risks, thereby avoiding stalls in comfort zones of the work and activity; 9) Evaluation, and that evaluation incorporates the ability to accept feedback and make self-corrections; and 10) Ownership, and that ownership incorporates a proprietary attitude toward one's own ideas and products.*

With those broad, meaningful brush strokes painting the portraits of leaders, and by implication, followers, the

---

* Charles A. Garfield, **Success**, April 1983.

following general narratives describing leaders and followers are helpful in understanding the nature of both. They also help us understand the dynamics implied in any leader/follower situation.

LEADER OF LEADERS. They are persons who want to lead, or at least feel inwardly driven to take on leadership responsibility. They not only believe they can lead, but significant other persons related to the circumstances also believe they can. Goal orientation is generally important to them, but they are not doctrinaire about goals. They have an ability to see whole situations, and hold them clearly when they are dealing with their parts.

Leaders of leaders delegate, listen, teach, inspire and create. They refuse to take project issues personally, a vital matter in maintaining objectivity, for objectivity is necessary to flexibility. Commonly they have more energy than others, more dynamism.

When purposes are clear, leaders of leaders sketch out strategies, communicate with participants, monitor progress, and evaluate both personnel and progress, making adjustments and amendments. On occasion they make summary decisions that may be wrong. They are not destroyed by failure. They are flexible to make mid-course corrections, and they seem to have the ability to fill in gaps that others leave. Even so, they appear unhurried, and they like to be careful enough to avoid making large or numerous amendments to projects in progress. They like to do what they do, right, the first time. They also are more concerned with doing the right things than with doing things right, as Drucker affirmed for modern leaders. Even so, if wrong approaches are made, the leader can amend them along the line.

With significant exceptions, leaders of leaders tend to share honors for achievements. Also with significant exceptions, these leaders often are free of need for personal honor. They seem to be at their best when they

FIGURE EIGHT

Four classifications of leaders/followers

1. Leaders of leaders	Goal oriented Inspirational, creative, charismatic Maintain objectivity Possess high energy levels Not destroyed by failure Willing to take risks
2. Leaders	Function to accomplish purposes of leaders of leaders Less charismatic than leaders of leaders Better managers of people, resources than leaders of leaders Concerned with feelings, welfare of followers Understand specific problems clearly High sense of duty
3. Followers	Need leaders to mobilize, organize and motivate them to achieve goals Open to direction, but like involvement in decision making Feel less responsible for projects Not as comfortable with risks as leaders Not as open to evaluation as leaders Are key to success
4. Followers of followers	Have time to fill or kill Feel no driving motivation Respond to whatever is available Not likely to think through purposes Like to be anonymous Sometimes participate through coercion or guilt

are brave to take responsibility, even blame, when subordinates fail. Sometimes subordinates are permitted to take blame for failure to protect the integrity of the leader of leaders. But the best of these leaders are confident persons, believing that even if they miss their ideal, another try at the current problem, or another cause, is worth the effort. Even though confident, the leader of leaders knows or senses his limitations. He does not succeed in every situation and with all types of personnel.

They, like the managers they need to gain their purposes, require little security. They do not expect tenure. They believe in themselves and what they can do. They buy stock in the company or believe truly in their flag.

LEADERS. They are persons who are skilled in important ways, competent in dealing with both people and issues, and useful to fulfill a service they can identify, or is identified to them. Sometimes they have more practical intelligence, the ability to think through matters in applicable formulations, than do leaders of leaders. But they generally do not have the personality, or charisma, or creativity found in leaders of leaders. Nor do they appear to be as interested in the philosophies of power, or ethics, or the like, as their mentors. They are often better managers of persons and organizations than charismatic leaders. Perhaps they ought to be called managers rather than leaders. But managing and leading are really the same thing, with some variance in emphases.

These leaders may handle budgets better, understand specific problems more clearly, and find fulfillment in completed tasks, well done. They can go far on recognition from their leader, the leader of leaders, and are less concerned with the approval of followers. Leaders function to accomplish the purposes of the leader of leaders, in large part because they identify those purposes as their own. They have a high sense of duty. They believe in their skills, knowing others look to them for identity with projects.

Even so, leaders are concerned with the feelings and welfare of followers. To carry through their effective supervision, leaders try to be visible to their people, even appearing on occasion to be one of them. There is, nevertheless, something extra that is commonly recognized as necessary to their leadership. They make practical the dreams of the creative man or woman above them. They are, in some ways, mother/father figures. They can and do sublimate their own needs and emotions for the good of others.

FOLLOWERS. They are persons who need leaders to accomplish purposes important to an institution, community or social order. They are, generally, competent people. Many are positive, affirming their leaders and themselves. They may not have the resources to accomplish large goals they like to identify and set. They do not know how to tackle all the problems. They need a leader, a mobilizer, an organizer to direct their energies and collect or assign resources. They know the meaning of corporate activity, giving up private, independent action for larger corporate activity with larger meaning.

Even when followers perceive their own leadership ability they may not wish to enervate themselves to use it in any extensive way. They prefer less publicity than leaders, although they expect and need recognition for what they do. They are somewhat open to being told what to do, but enjoy also being a part of the decision making process. They find more emotional than intellectual ties with purposes. They feel less responsible for the project, and cords are neither so strong nor so tightly drawn as they are for leaders. They are not as comfortable with risks as leaders are. Evaluation is not as easily accepted as leaders accept it. This suggests a lower confidence in themselves than that found in leaders.

Followers are not likely willing to take responsibility for failure, but they like some identification with success related to their work. At their best, followers are humble to serve leaders in order to accomplish worthy ends. They know that, for the good of the order, leaders are needed, and leaders need them. If committed to the cause, followers serve sacrificially and are key to success.

FOLLOWERS OF FOLLOWERS. They are the remaining persons in the society, or community, or institution. They have time to fill or kill. They may be swept along with tides, or dawdle through experiences, feeling no driving motivation for this purpose. They are the pedestrians, the mass. They tend to respond to whatever is available. Their commitments are tenuous, their beliefs are soft. They are less occupied than more dynamic followers or leaders, less likely to think through the purposes of their lives. They like to be anonymous, and only periodically will participate in anything new. They feel casual about things. They do some things because they feel coerced, or intimidated, or even ashamed. Life is not demanding, or so they feel, and expectations are not to be taken seriously.

Followers of followers may include representatives from all personality types. They may be hard-working, perhaps simple, and uncomplicated in their life approach. They may be serious, shy men and women preoccupied with their own matters, but willing to grant modest energy to the friend-follower or friend-leader. They may be frivolous, desiring few if any commitments in life. They follow today because they have nothing better to do. Whatever is available is today's ball game. They may be theoretical idealists, even intellectuals, disillusioned and disappointed with former projects they have known. They feel some compulsion, but not a great deal. They may be drafted into a project. On occasions some followers of followers seem to go along with a project but conduct themselves in a manner that is destructive to the purpose. Seeming to identify, they actually serve to destroy. By identifying with a project in some modest way, predicting its failure, they can destroy the project in a self-fulfilling prophecy. There are others, however, who feel the motivation of leaders and followers and emerge to participate with energy and enthusiasm. They may determine the difference between victory and defeat for a project.

The matter of leading and following is complex, dynamic, mysterious and intriguing. It changes with changing circumstances and culture.

—8—

The Person of Leadership
LEADERS

And they come again to Jerusalem; and as he was walking in the temple, there come to him the chief priests, and the scribes, and the elders.

And they say to him, By what authority doest thou these things? and who gave thee this authority to do these things?

And Jesus answered and said unto them, I will also ask of you one question, and answer me, and I will tell you by what authority I do these things.

The baptism of John, was it from heaven, or of men? answer me.

And they reasoned with themselves, saying, if we shall say, From heaven; he will say, Why then did ye not believe him?

But if we shall say, Of men, they feared the people for all men counted John, that he was a prophet indeed.

And they answered and said unto Jesus, We cannot tell. And Jesus answering saith unto them, Neither do I tell you by what authority I do these things.

—Mark 11:27-33

Although we would often like to do so, we cannot separate leadership from the person of a leader. This compatibility of leader as person and function is primary to any view of Christian leadership. Forced to look at who a leader-person is, we seek information about his strengths and idiosyncrasies, his personality and how he functions as a leader. But clusters of factors become difficult to analyze or isolate because studies of leaders show ranges of clusters. A personality pattern cannot be prescribed for all leaders because no clear one emerges. However, some things do surface that alert us to leader characteristics we subscribe, and to those we reject.

In the passage from Mark's gospel cited above, we learn something about leaders in the differences of their persons. Chief priests, scribes and elders, presumably leaders, approached Jesus with questions. Apparently these were leaders representing a contingent. They held hidden agendas. They appear to have been prepared, their questions well formed. We know from other passages that their motives were unsatisfactory. They came not to learn truth, not to discover ways for leading their people into truth, new or old, but in some way to stop Jesus. To end this threat to their leadership required of them either authority with power or leadership with persuasion. They tried persuasion. Persuasion is the way of peace. Their strategy was to elicit answers from Jesus either to make Him appear heretical to the masses or trick Him into violating religious or legal limits in His affirmations. If they could reduce the message or the Man, they would achieve their purpose. His threat to them through His early success might come to an end, they believed. He would be exposed.

Jesus evaded being caught up in their web. Timing is vital to any leader—to Jesus, in the case here—and this was not the time to slap down a gauntlet. Jesus' strategy was to promise answer to their questions about His authority if they would respond clearly to His question. He, too, adopted rhetorical strategy. He then asked about the authority of John the Baptist. Was it from heaven or from men?

These leaders in Israel, in this exchange, recognized their forensic problem. They were about to lose a debate and could not find a way to turn it to victory. If they were to say John is of God, then Jesus would level them in rebuttal, revealing their failure to respond affirmatively to John. They would be exposed as hypocrites. If they denied the genuineness of John, they might be able to sustain a logical debate, for logic is not necessarily a tool of truth alone. But if they did, they would fall into political trouble because the people whom they wished to cultivate and whose support was vital to them believed in John. They assessed that they had better be neutral. To confess suspended intellectual judgment, they left open any possibility. The verdict on John, for them, was still out. They might not incur anyone's wrath with that delaying tactic. Their answer was that they did not know the reply to His question. When they refused to commit themselves, Jesus turned attention from Himself by also withholding information. In point of fact, Jesus' strategy maintained His own time schedule. He was able, but not yet willing, to confront these leaders on divine authority in living prophets.

THE LEADER AND HIS PERSONAL RIGHTS

The leader is always the object of prejudice from uninformed people, and the object of opposition from others who perceive matters differently from him. The first commonly oppose the man, the second commonly oppose his viewpoint. The leader's hope is to keep prejudice sufficiently at a minimum or dampened so that he may do his work. He feels some obligation to meet his opposition on principle. He must resist the urge to self-defense. To meet the opposition sucks up valuable time. Answers must be carefully chosen, well directed, if they are used at all.

In all of nature, imperfect as it is, contradictory forces are at work. Resistance to human effort is in the nature of things. A tree sprouts and sends its roots downward. There appears to be nothing but rock. Nevertheless, the tree survives if it is tough and can find nourishment. The scarcity of nourishment is the problem. The rock is a barrier to the source of nourishment. The tree "fights" the rock. It is smaller than other trees nearby that do not grow on rocks. It is stunted by comparison to the tree it might have become. Even though it may split, the rock remains with the tree. In time of storm the tree in the rock may survive longer than larger trees in soil. There are compensations. Two sets of circumstances prevail. We cannot say which is superior until we discover what purpose is valuable to us.

Perhaps leaders must have resistance to test them, to create tension for the purpose of control. In any event, leaders must know that resistance to their leadership will be common. It will last as long as the leader is active, and perhaps longer. Some of the resistance is accounted for in the differences in good people, the way they think. They follow their own style in doing things, and their own order of activities. They are compelled, by human nature, to

question a person's course, perhaps question the integrity
of the person.

But some resistance is due to negative factors. Jealousy
is common. Other leaders, or would-be leaders, followers
of other leaders or other points of view, will resist in any
way they can. Impugning motives, fabricating stories, or
creating *non sequitur* objections become commonplace.
Hopefully, effective leaders feel strong to survive them.

Leaders should not be personally too sensitive. They
generally dare not slash back at detractors or disillusioned
followers. A follower easily finds rationalization for not
doing a duty. One of the easiest ways is to bring
accusation against the leader—distort statements, focus
on some triviality, or allege some failure. The leader
maintains his direction by refusing diversion when he
experiences no substantive resistance from detractors. He
refuses to get caught up in trivialities.

THE LEADER AND HIS RISKS

Leaders may not succeed. Perhaps for every successful
leader there is at least one unsuccessful. For each
baseball team manager who wins, another loses. For
every military general in the field who wins, another
loses. The belief that equates leadership with success and
winning is false faith.

Risk is integral to leadership. Risk taking as a quality
for a leader seems to be waning as an evaluative and
acceptable element. Near certainty is a benefit to be
sought. All matters are to be reviewed and covered before
projects are launched. But certainty is an illusion. Some
risk is necessary in most situations. The larger a matter,
the more significant may be the risk. Leaders who are
power oriented, who see life in a win/lose experience,
generally possess significant tolerances for risk. When
apprised of the Spanish galleon force at Trafalgar, Lord
Nelson placed a telescope to his blind eye and reported

seeing nothing of the Spanish. To the individualist, the win/lose man, the "Nelson gesture" is fraught with greatness. Nelson won. Had he lost the battle, he might have been reported an idiot for the blind eye "look" at the enemy. His gesture might have become an illustration of buffoonery.

Dramatic illustrations of win/lose in leadership could be cited. A young Winston Churchill nearly closed his life career because of his inept actions in the Boer War. He floundered, but learned lessons so as not to fail in the same way again. One author argued that even in losing in that early experience Churchill revealed "genius." He later risked himself in the House of Commons on military preparedness and resistance to Hitler. When war came, he was a hero.

Leaders fail for many reasons. They may be the wrong leaders for the current problem. Time or tragedy may work against them. Some, moving along well, see their support systems pulled away. Events turn against them. Others lose because even greater and more creative strategists appear, sometimes in opposition. A leader may arrive too soon, or too late. Woodrow Wilson was partly ahead of his time. Abraham Lincoln was on time. Oliver Wendell Holmes was perceived to be too old when an opening appeared to become Chief Justice. Dwight Eisenhower found time on his side in war, and later in peace. Neville Chamberlain, whose trust was violated by Adolph Hitler, paved the way for Winston Churchill's immortality. Churchill was, in turn, aided by the decline of Adolph Hitler and, perhaps, the weather over the English Channel. The western allies were ready when Churchill needed them. Many students of leadership ascribe "luck" as a large factor in analyzing leadership and success. It is a hard factor to understand and explain.

Jouvenal described two basic types of leaders. The first is the DUX, or the creative leader. He is an activist and an innovator. He feels he must bring something new to a situation or he is not leading.

The second is the REX, or the managing leader. He is a stabilizer and organizer. He tends to consolidate gains, and feels a need to perfect innovations, perhaps innovations introduced by his predecessor, a DUX leader. He may dislike the DUX, whom he criticizes as "woolly-headed." The DUX may dislike the REX as one who takes advantage of achievements to which he made no original contribution. DUX believes REX to be lacking in originality and creativity. But REX is needed sooner

---

FIGURE NINE

Types of leaders

DUX leader vs. REX leader	DUX is a creative leader, an activist and innovator who feels he must bring something new to a situation. DUX may criticize REX for lack of originality, creativity. REX is a managing leader who stabilizes, organizes, consolidates gains and perfects innovations. REX may criticize DUX as "woolly-headed."
Advocate leader	Sacrifices himself for a cause.
Consensus leader	Implements strategies through consensus.
Manager leader	Has ability to manage people, resources.
Charismatic leader	Inspires followers to achievement.
Theoretical leader	Exerts influence through ideas.

or later to manage things. *

Various types of leaders emerge, succeeding or failing, created by other causes than those found alone in the person of the leader. Several additional factors are vital. For example, there is the *advocate leader*, like Martin Luther King, Jr. King became a symbol through speeches and public self-sacrifice, putting himself in critical but dangerous situations. It was time for a man like King. Intelligent enough to cast his views in clear and appealing language, King accomplished more that other black leaders of his era. Not only did he use the full arsenal of advocacy (modern rhetoric, personal risk, role model, public righteousness), he used them with great skill. The situation was right for him, and King selected events to be accented. He was astute in analyzing the social climate.

Dwight David Eisenhower was a *consensus leader*. He learned staff patterns as a military man. Although military officers are sometimes characterized as autocratic and "going by the book," they are well-disciplined to work through consensus viewpoints, and become firm advocates of these plans and decisions. The best leaders bring originality to the agreed-upon strategies. They know the goal and seek its achievement, either through plan or improvisation.

Herbert Hoover was a *manager leader*. Schooled as an engineer, Hoover quickly made his world reputation in oil. His ability to manage people and resources was recognized, and he was drawn into public service. Following World War I, he demonstrated remarkable organizational skill to feed starving Europe. He was invited to serve in the cabinet of President Warren Harding. As Secretary of Commerce he was highly effective in setting up agencies like the Interstate Communication Commission for the emerging radio

---

* "Leadership: The Biggest Issue," **Time Magazine**, November 8, 1976, p. 31.

industry, a commission that remains in place in government today with expanded scope including television. Hoover was untouched by scandal that racked the Harding administration. He was elected President of the United States in 1928. Unprecedented prosperity appeared to need a manager. Within a year the Great Depression struck the United States and the world.

The magnificent manager failed because the country needed an inspirational leader with charisma, someone who would bring inspiration and hope to people. The population turned to Franklin D. Roosevelt. Neville Chamberlain, a manager type, yielded belatedly to Winston Churchill, a charismatic. In Germany, Von Hindenburg, a manager type, yielded to Hitler, a charismatic. This is not to say that the Nazi was like a Democrat, but to say that managers yielded to charismatic leaders.

There are, also, *theoretical leaders*. They live in the long historical shadows of Plato and Socrates. Plato loved the idea of the philosopher-king. In the twentieth century men like Robert Maynard Hutchins, Albert Einstein and John Dewey were theoretical leaders. They wished to be activists in some acceptable way, and accomplished some activism, but were largely influential through their ideas and the persons touched by them. Hutchins, at thirty years of age, was invited to the presidency of the University of Chicago. From that office, for many years, he wrote and delivered speeches, influenced curricula, argued for his ideas and challenged future educationists. He closed his life with lowered profile in a "think tank" in Santa Barbara, California, largely supported by profits from the sales of a popular sex manual prepared by a friend. Theoretical leaders are not easily evaluated. But their influence, which is one form of leadership, is acknowledged to be significant.

The modern Church has been greatly influenced by

theoretical leaders, especially by theologians in Europe. Barth, Brunner, and the several score scholarly theologians emerging after World Wars I and II, have had unmistakable effect upon the Church, liberal and conservative.

Leaders are sometimes classified by their motivations. *Power* motivation has been a leading force for many. Numerous analysts believe virtually all leadership has some power motivation in it. Richard M. Nixon appears to have made power central in his administration of the American presidency. Many men at the center of his team were, by their own admission, power oriented men. Power appears to man to be both glamorous and dangerous. The drive to gain and hold power is strong despite personal dangers accruing to those who gain it.

Achievement motivation is high among educational leaders. They feel good about writing books, addressing influential bodies, and knowing that they control areas of human activity because of their knowledge. Artists, like actors and musicians, gain prestige to leadership from what they do and the publicity they receive. Even athletes can assert that leadership.

Affiliate motivation is sometimes strong but seems, on occasion, to be flimsy at base. President Jimmy Carter was in difficulty almost from the beginning of his administration because of "cronyism." They were "the good old boys," perhaps beyond their depth in managing a great and complex nation. A man of high integrity, the president did not use the force of his character to accomplish his purposes. In that omission he appeared to avoid his strongest point for leadership.

Spiritual motivation is highest when it most fully seeks the glory of God. Jesus held that motivation. But so did others in the Bible, like Job, Melchizedek, Moses, Deborah, Samuel and Abigail. In many ways genuine spiritual motivation is most ideal because it provides fewest self-interests in it. It relies heavily on the character and human quality of the leader. It is the kind of leadership that is longest remembered in history. Lists of the most influential personages in history include more names in this category (religion) than we might have guessed.

The above suggests that there may well be different leaders to meet different needs. To incorporate wrong leadership in a situational context may create the illusion that there is no leadership. Perhaps the best leader can do some of all that is needed. But can he do them all well? Vital to him is the recognition on his part that there is more than one kind of leadership. He may need to draft others who will make up his omissions.

THE LEADER AND HIS ISSUES

The idealistic leader tends to maintain and practice principles of problem solving and developing human relationships. He seldom violates objectivity to yield to the pressures and vicissitudes of the people and circumstances around him. He establishes his objectivity as soon as feasible, proving he is fair and even-handed. It is assumed that leaders, like other people, are not always objective, that they will on occasion show favoritism, and that they will sometimes improve their own situations at the expense of men and women under their leadership. They tend to take perquisites of privilege. That human beings do act in ways that benefit themselves through exploitation of others, others not fully aware of what they are doing, has been well documented.

Leaders are sometimes unseated because it is believed that they know what to do to avoid further human problems and do not do it. It is believed that they know more than they do, sometimes more than they can. A school principal, trying to solve a problem involving surly and active youths, was challenged by the community of parents because of alleged mishandling of the case, a case larded over with racial prejudice and presumed wrong strategies in the treatment of the boys. It was shown that none of the alleged factors appeared, but the vocal group admittedly used the case as means for attracting attention to their concerns. Their high motives for better social justice were supported by their own unethical means for leadership. They exploited a situation with the rationale that the end justifies the means.

Despite any injustice done him in a situation, an effective leader maintains his objectivity. He does so, even recognizing the lack of objectivity in his enemies, or even in his followers. His life can become complicated, if he permits himself to run to his own defense. He knows things are not even. He can do his best and things go wrong. Some of his ideals may be diluted in inexorable events. But he knows what the world is like. He keeps equilibrium. He will lead again. But if he does not he has been involved in the "real" world that gives and takes. He can lose and feel good about having been involved.

In his focus the leader must be clear to himself. He does this in part because he wishes to live with the venture through to the end. But he cannot be sure. One of the most forlorn experiences one will ever observe in life is to see a person who inaugurated and built a meaningful project cut off from it. He fades even while his work flourishes. He may have failed at some point in leadership, or he may have been usurped. His protection against such an event is to maintain clear focus on the main task. He glories in the results of his dream, even if as dreamer he is isolated from the project. He refuses to permit side issues, especially those that would relate to him personally, to intervene in an ultimate achievement. Somewhere in the order of God there will appear equity for him. He leaves the matter there.

Another reason for focus on issues is so that the leader

(or follower, for that matter) may explain what he is about to his family, perhaps also to influential friends. He needs them. So he may even mobilize them for his task while they guard him against his own excesses and potential errors. They can understand why, for a period of time, he is driven to accomplish this purpose.

The sharper the focus, the better able the leader will be to recruit personnel and solicit resources. He needs help, help from lowly workers to wealthy philanthropists. They dare not be fooled. They cannot misunderstand. If they do their support will soften, or dissolve. If they are played the fool at the beginning, they will discover the ploy in due time. The end of that leader and his project may be worse than the beginning, a beginning that started without reality.

An important reason then to intensify focus is to be better able to defend the purpose, especially during difficult times. The leader wishes to maintain his momentum, to be sure the work is ongoing.

In leadership focus the person finds himself and clarifies his part as leader:

1) *Setting goals*. This is carefully done. Written, those goals are amenable to amendment, so they may enlarge, shrink, change, or in some adaptation serve as guides to the future.

2) *Selecting pertinent information*. This is to separate fact from fiction and rumor. What is the reality of the situation? What may be passed over? What cannot be passed over? Many questions must be answered, and sources documented.

3) *Persuading followers to participate*. The leader asks for two large commitments from followers: the giving of themselves to serve, and the commitment of themselves in loyalty. An appeal to emotions and motives must be effective. The follower gives enough, neither too little nor too much, but enough. If he gives too little, the project

may flounder. If he gives too much, he may retreat from so large duty. Persuasion appears historically to have been one of the abilities highly prized by leaders. The apostle Paul mastered persuasion, not only for preaching, but to extricate himself from threatening circumstances (Acts 23:6-10).

4) *Risking himself.* In risking himself the leader proves to followers that he and his purpose are genuine. Jesus clearly took the risk. In the end, when taken and tried for His words, He opened the way for His followers to escape, to save themselves. At first uncertain, the eleven surviving disciples followed through to the end of their lives. They, too, were willing to risk. And they paid the ultimate price of life, life itself. For many persons, such sacrifice is asking too much. For disciples the benefits more than make up for the supreme risk of self.

5) *Communicating necessary information.* Without satisfactory communication a movement will not sustain itself. But not everything is to be communicated. Only that which is necessary. Only that which is relevant—true and plausible. Knowing how easily the public can be fooled, and how embarrassing it is to find oneself

---

FIGURE TEN

Steps to leadership focus

1. Setting goals
2. Selecting pertinent information
3. Persuading followers to participate
4. Risking himself
5. Communicating necessary information
6. Developing a sense of timing
7. Providing a plan to meet situational needs
8. Looking for divine guidance

exploited, the leader provides enough information for thoughtful action. Jesus, as He approached the conclusion of His ministry, insisted on providing information about His death and resurrection. Most analysts might well have discouraged His briefings. The disciples clearly did not like what He said on the point. They appear to have blanked out His teachings about His own ordeal, death and recovery. After the death and resurrection they were partly settled on the meaning of the course of events by recalling their conversations with Jesus. He had not misled them.

6) *Developing a sense of timing*. The leader who is best at what he does coordinates all factors. All is ready as a scheduled matter. Delay is avoided. Needs are met on time, as they are anticipated. Jesus is partly known to us in a special treatment of time. He came "in the fullness of time." He was revealed to His disciples and to Israel in His time. His death was calculated to the Passover. His resurrection was stated to span a period equivalent to Jonah's ordeal with the great fish. Christians, His followers, live with the promise of His return, on a schedule known to Him.

7) *Providing a plan to meet the needs*. Through plans, strategies, projections, personnel, the leader confronts the special problem to be solved. Calling upon resources, human and natural, he leads toward a goal. He is competent to do what must be done.

8) *Looking for divine guidance*. The Christian feels that prayer and an awareness of dependence upon God are vital to his commitment either as a leader or follower for life course. The more intent is this "God-consciousness," in its right sense, the greater becomes one's humility, but also the greater the authority to function. It is a meekness, as with Moses, not a weakness, as with King Saul.

—9—

The Pattern of Leadership
SUMMARY

Let a man regard us in this manner, as servants of Christ…it is required of stewards that one be found trustworthy. But to me it is a very small thing that I should be examined by you, or by any human court; in fact, I do not even examine myself. I am conscious of nothing against myself, yet I am not by this acquitted; but the one who examines me is the Lord.

—1 Cor. 4:1-4

For if you were to have countless tutors in Christ, yet you would not have many fathers; for in Christ Jesus I became your father through the gospel. I exhort you therefore, be imitators of me.

—1 Cor. 4:15-16

F acing up to oneself is a major problem for anyone, especially evaluating objectively his attitudes, competencies, knowledge, energy levels, personality and moral character. But facing up is necessary if he is to confront successfully either his own problems or those of the institution he represents. If he does confront himself in meaningful ways, he can sense his improvement. Improvement may create appropriate euphoria in him. He feels good about himself and what he is doing.

Simple patterns for self-evaluation and perception may be designed. Continua from 0 to 100 may be drawn, and each factor scored from poor (0), to fair (25), to good (50), to excellent (75), to superior (100). There are obvious gradations between these fixed points for evaluation. The following are some factors to evaluate as they relate to the prospective leader or follower. In their hope for effectiveness, both the leader and follower need to understand the dynamic patterns possible to them. The individual should find himself, as leader and follower.

How does he relate to *change*?

Change, as noted earlier, occurs inevitably but at varying speeds or rates. If slow enough, change can be managed by most people. But the rate of change is accelerating in a technological society, dominated by media and finance. Changes multiply while time frames narrow. There is evidence that many men and women are unable to absorb great change in short space.

To encounter change is to experience tension even when change is perceived to be beneficial. A community of citizens called together to evaluate a proposal to construct a new building in their neighborhood may be convinced of the value of the addition (change). The citizens speak in support of the plan, and vote resoundingly in its favor. As excavation begins, tension begins to rise in the community. On occasion persons who voted for the proposal enter legal objections in an attempt to stop the project. They are often unsure of why they now object to what they formerly approved, or why they formerly approved what they now reject.

In small ways we can discover how change affects us. A friend may change his grooming habits, his style of haircut, and growth of a beard. Or weight changes greatly impress his friends. His friends inevitably react affirmatively or negatively. No matter how they react, something has happened that is slightly discomforting. They are not sure either of their friend or themselves. They feel that whatever they say, even if favorable, will be the wrong thing.

To welcome change requires affirmative, even adventuresome, attitudes. Confidence is strong in people who welcome and accept change. This does not mean they believe change is necessarily good. They know that change can be very damaging indeed. Change must justify itself. The status quo need not. *What is* holds the field. Change carries the burden of proof. When sufficient proofs are in, and change is indicated, it ought to be generated.

Agreeable with man and society or not, change will occur, sometimes in dramatic ways. During the years since 1970, the change in industry has been dramatic beyond the comprehension of most workers. Many refused the change from goods to services as the future for employment. Machine robots were designed to fabricate automobiles, roll out steel, and build tires. United States Steel was replaced by McDonald's Golden Arches as symbol of American business. Rolling sheet metal became less lucrative than frying hamburgers. Change from typewriters to word processors, from drawing boards to computers and the like became more than some persons could take.

In general, men and women give favorable lip service to change. They identify change with youth, and they wish to "think young." In reality they commonly withhold themselves and their resources so that change does not really take place, or its pace is dramatically slowed. They are surprised to discover that even young generations, with all their protests notwithstanding, are also threatened by change when that change touches them. Change is not the profile of youths: it is the profile of the adventurous, the risk taker, at any age.

How does he relate to *goals*?

Goals, related to large purposes, are cast in long and short range terms. They include time frames, objectives, and activities to accomplishment. Through goal setting one is enabled to guide change, both in specific objectives and within an acceptable time period.

To become a goal setter a person commonly is forced to shift his approach to life, persons, things and himself. He may find a new psychology for living. Formerly he tended to react, to respond to whatever is immediate, and thereby to survive the day. He functions on the basis of what happened, a series of pleasant accidents. At least the great volume of events is pleasant enough for each person.

Projection of life activity, deliberately and carefully designed, replaces personal reaction and accident for the goal setter. The future becomes the arena for activity rather than settings from either an irretrievable past or the tyrannical present. To set goals promptly and practically in order to assure early success encourages further goal setting. But leaders must further, perhaps faster, move beyond this vestibule of planning.

Leaders organize a case for planning. They fix their sights when they have stock of their resources—personnel, environment, opportunity—and when all are presumed to be in place, or have reasonable promise to be—they announce their meanings. They know further that resources and support will likely increase when goals are set and some action has been taken. Goals must be balanced with each other to compose a total plan. Generally two or three goals are not sufficient to build a case, if the cause includes at least a group. Personal goals for individuals may be few and simple.

Backgrounding goals are answers to crucial questions in the life of an individual, and the adaptation of these answers to the institution he represents. As discussed earlier in this writing, a philosophy of life exists in each person. It becomes useful and helpful when it is comprehensive. So it must be written. It will be, and ought to be, amended from time to time. It becomes a guide, perhaps a reminder of how things are perceived, and provides some idea about how life is to be encountered by and for the author. If it is well formed the philosophy deserves high and intensive commitment. Without commitment life and ideas separate too often and too far. The loss of commitment is a common and major weakness in most persons. In the loss, goals fade.

How does this covenant emerge? It should include at the outset a summary about large issues of belief in God (or to the contrary for nontheists, in some humanism), and in democratic processes (or to the contrary as Ayn Rand would have it, in radical individualism). It should include views about family and other institutions, and a perception of self. Questions must be answered in straightforward statements: What are the important issues in my life? What are the practical matters? (These include the occupation, education, family, lifestyle, and the like that I wish to include in my experience). What are my personal strengths or attributes? (These should be ranked from strongest to least strong.) What are my weaknesses or omissions? (These, too, should be ranked from least strategic shortcoming to omissions.) What do I like to do most? We know that what a person likes to do, he does best. (Again, ranking will be helpful to reduce later competition in any pursuit of the items.) What do I dislike to do most? (Ranking may be necessary sooner or later because most persons will have to do some things they dislike doing, and they may have a choice, if they are clear about life patterns.)

Out of this grist I can project my whole life. My own computation has been to project to standard retirement age, 65 years, and add fifteen years. The fifteen have been divided into the first ten and the last five. These are the time measurements for my life purposes and goals.

Long term goals, for me, are usually between three years and five years, and relate closely to my life purposes. They include the majors: spiritual, intellectual, professional, family, and financial matters. They can readily be adjusted or amended. For example, I could carry them through as a professional, a college president, a minister, a teacher, a counselor, or a consultant. To move from one to the other I would make only slight shifts in personal goals, with large ones in the professional area relating to the actual situation that emerges. But the process would remain dynamic and work well.

Short term goals for me are one- to three-year projections, very specifically determined. At the time of this writing I have completed four three-year terms in administration at a college, and have been invited to consider another term. The invitation accepted, I am in the process of casting the goal pattern for the next three years.

How does he relate to *time*?

Time is a primary resource in the achievement of goals. All goals must be cast in time frames. Purposes are not so specific. Objectives have to do with achieving the goal. A purpose may be to upgrade my home. My goal might be to reroof the house by October 1 of this current year. The objectives are to include planning, contracting, financing, and whatever other activities may be necessary to achieve the goal. Without the time frame, between this date and October 1, I cannot know success. Success is measured by a goal (finish line) and the time it takes to reach that goal (a mile in four minutes).

Comparing scheduled lives to unscheduled is interesting business. Those who make such studies agree unanimously that scheduled people nearly always win. Those who permit circumstances to drive them are not, as a rule, the movers in society, or in their group. They tend to be less satisfied with their lives and accomplishments than persons who plan. Casual men and women often appear to be happy and pleased with their circumstances. Their very casualness and glibness with life are sometimes cover-up for disappointment with what they believe is life's deal. That deal seems ordinary to them, or even to have determined their failure.

To treat time as a commodity is an advanced viewpoint in civilization. The perception came with human sophistication. Population masses perceived time after kings and princes learned its secrets. A study of the history of time perceptions is an entrancing review of man, his ideas about himself, and his effectiveness in society. Time can be bought and sold, wasted or used beneficially, held in short or long supply, but whatever is lost cannot be recovered. Our fight with time is an evidence of human depravity, or more correctly, depravity's partial result. One of the biblical evidences that creation will be restored in its ideal state will be that a man will live long enough to use up his productivity (Isaiah 65).

Leaders learn that only so much time should be expended for a task. If a duty can be carried through in this time frame, it is worth the effort. By such means quantitative decisions are made (1 Cor. 16:12). By such means some pyrrhic time "victories" are avoided.

What are his *priorities*?

By setting priorities one lists his values and the order of importance for the activities that use up his lifetime. No one can do everything his imagination conceives for him to do. He is finite, but his mind projects the infinite. He must sift out even his own suggestions to find what is best for him.

Priorities inevitably reveal values. Some sophisticated teachers have denied that they make value judgments, but an astute analyst will discern values and judgments in sifting out their priorities. There are things that come first, second, third in his life. He may not be conscious of the order, but it is there and can be codified by astute analysts.

To set priorities is to suggest means for gaining order in one's life. Because my life is a very important thing to me, I must set my personal priorities to be satisfied with that life. For me, in general priorities, God is first, my wife is next, my children, parents and relatives follow in some family hierarchy, and my work is fourth. Other priorities follow at a rapidly reducing rate of importance, like recreation and social activity. When asked how he developed those great football teams in Green Bay, the eminent coach, Vince Lombardi, said that he instilled faith, family and football into his players, and in that order. He believed a man played better football if genuine faith and a loving family were higher motivations. Football was not worth the first place. It would be played better by those who put it in third place if God and family occupied first and second positions.

After general priorities are determined, specified ones can be set. For example, when I have fixed my professional position, and cast it in the large pattern of my life, what is the specific pattern for it? When do I go to work? How long will I work? What time slot will go to answering mail? How much time will be private? How much public? Whom will I see, and for how long a time? What is the place for planning in this assignment? What will I delegate, and why? When everything is "rightly put together" the priorities have been set.

One of my administrative techniques is to assign three, four or five large duties to an administrator, and suggest in the assignment what is the most through to the least important duty. If he works down through four, and asserts that the fifth is too much, then the fifth may be lifted. But before it is, we analyze what is happening in the four getting attention. He may prefer the fifth priority and drop the third. Another person may prove to be excellent for number three but uncertain with number five. We then reorder priorities.

How does he *plan*?

Planning is necessary to assure maintenance of priorities. Things done properly do not just happen. To develop a strategy one must analyze the circumstances related to the project. In this step, history may be important. What events and causes brought us to this point? What strategy can be designed to move us forward?

When the strategy has been perceived, and the plan set through careful involvement of the people who must carry out the plan, the tasks are assigned and monitoring is begun. Evaluation techniques are agreed upon and methods of procedure are set. Ideally, responsibility is taken and carried by all who participate.

The leader is involved. He can easily interfere, and he can easily neglect. He can fail by assigning loners to groups, and persons with excellent interpersonal skills to individual assignments. He can reward in such a manner that honors have no substance, his ways appearing saccharine and insincere. Or credits appear so seldom that he appears insensitive and disinterested.

Successful leaders learn about people and planning by working with people and plans. What went wrong? What went right? Why did some persons working together accomplish so much? Why did others fail either in single or multiple assignments? And so the analysis continues, until patterns emerge to be used in the next opportunity.

What is his attitude toward *self*?

Esteem for oneself is important if that person is to be consistently effective. To accept one's own physical being is a portent for his success and personal happiness. Accepting himself, his age, sex, life, health, limitations will determine much about how he will be accepted by others. During much of my adult life I have observed persons who have "two strikes against them," but who were effective because they perceived their own worth realistically. They refused either to accept prejudice *as it was, or could have been applied to them*. They belonged to minority races, to other social groups, to unacceptable families, to small religious societies, to an unpopular age group, to a group with physical limitations. This last included the female sex in male-dominated bastions.

Persons need to know that they will not lose in life because of some socially unattractive and prejudicial factor or factors, if they do not lose to themselves. When an individual has something substantive to offer, his personal disadvantages, or what are taken as disadvantages, are of no great moment. To be too young, too old, too fat, too short, too bald, too much of anything, will not be too great disadvantage if all else is in order, and if the individual does not sell himself short.

To accomplish adequate levels of self-esteem one should cultivate his spiritual potential. Rightly understood, spiritual growth in an individual must be the best way to build a sense of worth. What could make me feel more valuable than to feel that God, with many things to do, cares for me and that I can maintain a personal relationship with Him? Persons who have no faith in God must perforce perceive themselves of less worth than enlightened believers in God. Without God I am an animal, no matter how advanced, no matter how intelligent. To disbelieve in the human spiritual dimension is to hold a different view of man and conduct than that held by a believer. Spiritual development relates to the improvement of the mind, to the feeding of spiritual hunger, to the heightening of awareness in all that is Christian, and to the maturing of the soul/spirit. In all of earth's creation only man, under God, can think, sense, feel and believe.

How does he *communicate*?

Communication is vital to the expression of self. It is vital to the leader in times of enlightenment when followers are, with the leader, aware of their growth. Persons made in the image of God, and holding self-esteem, should not be treated as property. They do rightly refuse to be so treated. They do not exist for the convenience of the leader or for the power structure. They should be informed about anything that involves them, be persuaded when action and belief must be joined, and be instructed about progress, changes, results. All this is difficult to accomplish. But we must try, if we mean to lead.

To communicate substance the leader should be aware of evidence. He ought to know what is required to prove a point. For example, there is a difference between opinion that is virtually meaningless, and that which is authoritative and valid. I may hold many opinions about matters known to me. Many of these freight no force of evidence, but gullible listeners sometimes grant them value. In contrast, a physician's opinions on a subject of medicine relative to his expertise are authoritative. The authoritative opinion comes from a person who has earned his right to speak on a particular subject, and is recognized for his expertise.

Ideas must be cast in understandable language, forming clear, authoritative opinions, relevant illustrations, valid statistics and appropriate comparisons. With logical sequences, supported by these proofs, the burden of the communicator can be carried in ethical persuasion and informative disclosure. A proper case is woven.

To make ideas effective through communication, the leader should practice being an effective person. That practice extends to everything in his life, but here we are interested in communication. To practice effectively means to learn and use the principles of listening. This means to be accurate, to recognize personal agendas, to differentiate among the purposes of listening. One may listen for social exchange that is recognition of persons present, communicating humane attitudes. Listening may be therapeutic for the purpose of emotional healing of communicators and demonstration of concern in listeners. It may be for information so that the listener may know the facts of a case or event. Finally, listening becomes critical for the purpose of making judgments about the value of the message, or to respond to its persuasive intent.

A person practices to become effective when he improves his language style, when he speaks with appropriate force and emotion, when he combines verbal and nonverbal communication to accomplish right purposes. He is committed, understands his audience (one or many persons) and he creates an environment for favorable response.

What is his response to *persons*?

Persons are the objects to whom communication is directed. My attitudes toward them ought to be empathic. To identify with others empathically tells me something about myself. Am I empathic, or only sympathetic? Sympathy is seeing myself in others and responding tenderly. Empathy is seeing the other person as he is, and accepting truth about him with humaneness, and identification with him. Empathy is larger, more practical, more important than sympathy. It requires sensitivity that is not judgmental even when the other person is wrong. Empathy permits difference.

Maturity is a key factor. Developing into a mature person is vital to the meaning of man on earth. An adult who is childish in his perceptions and conduct cannot lead. The mature person refuses the melodramatic postures in himself, and he knows what they are, and are likely to accomplish in others. Many presumed leaders have high regard for the human race, but they don't like people.

Maturity exercises significant reduction in emotional responses, responses that are caused by real or alleged conduct in others. A mature man and woman can sustain their own composure when others around them are losing theirs. Anger is not met with anger, reprisal does not follow attack. Maturity gives one the ability to bear accusation and misunderstanding without retaliation.

What is his *motivation*?

Motivation is a compelling drive to do something, and that drive leads to action. If there is no action there is no genuine motivation. Without action the compelling drive becomes a fantasy. To identify drives is to find immediate causes for doing things. Persons do what they do to earn money, to become creative, to be appreciated, to find status, to fulfill service dedication to complete duty, to satisfy pride, to sustain a good feeling or result. Habit is a special kind of motivation, even though it is common. Persons are sometimes motivated to conduct themselves in certain ways because habit drives them. They may do something they dislike, like smoking tobacco, because the habit motivation has become strong. But habit may also serve to develop high levels of conduct.

Motives vary widely. Love for money takes one man: a fulfillment in service takes another. Persons following one motive pattern are commonly suspicious of those following another. Working with persons highly motivated by money rewards, an analyst confronts doubts from his audience when he touts service as a primary motivation. For example, some studies show high satisfaction among low-paid, service-oriented professionals. An example was reported in *Christianity Today* in 1977:

The average British clergyman's salary is only $4250 per year, but a magazine that conducted a survey on job satisfaction concluded that British ministers as a class are the men most satisfied with their jobs. Nearly 60 percent of the clergy among 24,000 persons polled said they were "very satisfied" in their work, and 86 percent said they would choose the same occupation again. The most miserable workers, according to the survey, were draftsmen.

Only 8 percent said they were happy in their jobs.*

In analyzing the unhappiness of athletes during the late 1970s and early 1980s, several writers and even athletes themselves attributed skyrocketing salaries for part of the decline in levels of satisfaction among players. The salaries became so important to professional sports that other motivations were diluted or neglected. As a result, professional sports appear to have changed somewhat from what they were. Games are no longer games. They are business. Champions are bought by ego-motivated owners of teams.

How salient are our beliefs about what we are doing? How strongly we follow our beliefs so that they generate our conduct is a test of what we are. If convictions weaken we may fail. We change. For some persons life, human and natural, is everything. Anything is permitted to assure survival for life. Unethical conduct is anything that would cost a life. In the end, for such persons, the desire to live is the great motivation. They would not serve as leaders for many projects. Their integrity would be lower quality than that of persons who will do right though the heavens fall.

Why a leader or follower is doing what he is doing, what his motivations are, may be the question of the moment.

How does he *evaluate*?

Evaluation is the discovery of the results of any activity and making or intimating a value judgment about those results. A leader is concerned to discover both personal and corporate progress or lack of it.

Personal evaluation may be done at various times in the course of events from daily reviews to larger time frames

---

* "World Scene," **Christianity Today,** November 4, 1977, p. 65.

through project points. Such evaluations may include both self-evaluations and those performed by others. This process is neither self-flagellation nor faultfinding. If it were, we would rightly shy away from it. Evaluation well formed includes references to excellence as well as areas needing improvement. The best reviews include suggestions for solving suggested problems.

When we have done a piece of work, states Desy Safan-Gerard, we must "stand back and assess coolly what has happened." Self-confrontations may demand changes, shifts, amendments. Safan-Gerard believes that, "while involvement in what we do is essential to creativity, we must also be detached enough to assess whether what we have done is fitting." Amateurs hold on to "irrelevancies and excesses." Safan-Gerard holds that self-indulgence is a common problem. Although her concern is with creativity, her perception about evaluation is sound for any context. She states as much: "Whether the end result is a painting, a report, or a reorganization plan, creativity occurs when there is successful

---

FIGURE ELEVEN

Factors for leadership evaluation

1. How does the leader relate to change?
2. How does the leader relate to goals?
3. How does the leader relate to time?
4. What are the leader's priorities?
5. How does the leader plan?
6. What is the leader's attitude toward self?
7. How does the leader communicate?
8. What is the leader's response toward persons?
9. What is his motivation?
10. How does the leader evaluate?

communication between a person and his work...something is perceived, elaborated, expressed and evaluated."*

Corporate evaluations follow similar patterns as personal ones. As much as possible reviews avoid statements that may be misconstrued as personal. What adjustments need to be made, additions and subtractions? Results will indicate whether or not goals should be speeded up or slowed, enlarged or reduced, assignments shifted in some ways, and resources added. The point to be made is that evaluation is not to ascertain right and wrong, except in moral issues, but to find what is effective and ineffective. Was the problem understood, was the solution appropriate and workable?

Certainly we may, in the name of evaluation, become carping critics. The loss for irresponsible faultfinding is incalculable. Was it not John Gardner who said that the nation suffers from uncritical lovers, and unloving critics? Our purpose is to solve problems, not to find fault. The leader is a problem solver. So is the follower.

Finally, leaders usually become effective leaders because they identify with a block of followers who identify with them. Keys to their effectiveness are the followers who provide workers, attitudes, commitments, resources and skills to accomplish purposes. Followers tend to gain the kind of leadership they are willing to support. Failure of leadership is often the failure of followership as Israel proved from time to time. Followers may require education for leadership loyalty and commitment.

The weaknesses of followers are the weaknesses of human nature. Those weaknesses are given in human

---

* Desy Safan-Gerard, "How to Unblock," **Psychology Today**, January 1978, p. 81.

life and institutions. Leaders are called upon to reduce the force of these negatives and lift ideas and activities to higher and more effective levels than they would be if leaders were not present. Leaders, then, must do more than followers, must provide model lives, must communicate, must give themselves, and must be, in the end, what they were called to be—leaders.

Bibliography

Alexander, John. *Managing Our Work*. Downers Grove, Ill.: InterVarsity Press. Rev. Ed. 1972.

Bolles, Richard Nelson. *What Color Is Your Parachute?* Berkeley, Calif.: Ten Speed Press, 1972.

Drucker, Peter F. *The Effective Executive*. New York: Harper & Row, 1966.

Engstrom, Ted W. and Edward R. Dayton. *The Art of Management for Christian Leaders*. Waco, Texas: Word Books, 1976.

Gerig, Donald. *Leadership in Crisis*. Ventura, Calif.: Regal Books, 1982.

Greenleaf, Robert K. *Servant Leadership*. New York: Paulist Press, 1977.

Griffin, Emory A. *Getting Together*. Downers Grove, Ill.: InterVarsity Press, 1982.

_____ *The Mind Changers*. Wheaton, Ill.: Tyndale House, 1976.

Johnson, James. *The Nine-to-Five Complex*. Grand Rapids, Mich.: Zondervan Publishing House, 1972.

LeTourneau, Richard. *Management Plus*. Grand Rapids, Mich.: Zondervan Publishing House, 1973.

Maccoby, Michael. *The Leader*. New York: Simon & Schuster, 1981.

Peters, Thomas J. and Robert H. Waterman, Jr. *In Search of Excellence*. New York: Harper & Row, 1982.

Rendall, Ted S. *Nehemiah: Laws of Leadership*. Three Hills, Alberta: Prairie Press, 1980.

Swindoll, Charles R. *Hand Me Another Brick*. Nashville, Tenn.: Thomas Nelson, Inc., 1978.